Eleutheria

by the same author

WAITING FOR GODOT
HAPPY DAYS
ENDGAME
COLLECTED SHORTER PLAYS
All That Fall, Act Without Words I, Act Without Words II,
Krapp's Last Tape, Rough for Theatre I, Rough for Theatre II,
Embers, Rough for Radio I, Rough for Radio II, Words and Music,
Cascando, Play, Film, The Old Tune, Come and Go, Eh Joe,
Breath, Not I, That Time, Footfalls, Ghost Trio, . . . but the
clouds . . . , A Piece of Monologue, Rockaby, Ohio Impromptu,
Quad, Catastrophe, Nacht und Träumen, What Where

HAPPY DAYS: SAMUEL BECKETT'S
PRODUCTION NOTEBOOK
(edited by James Knowlson)

THE THEATRICAL NOTEBOOKS OF SAMUEL BECKETT
General Editor: James Knowlson

Vol. I: Waiting for Godot
Edited by Dougald McMillan and James Knowlson

Vol. II: Endgame
Edited by S. E. Gontarski

Vol. III: Krapp's Last Tape
Edited by James Knowlson

SAMUEL BECKETT

Eleutheria

Translated from the French
by Barbara Wright

faber and faber
LONDON · BOSTON

First published in 1996
by Faber and Faber Limited
3 Queen Square London WC1N 3AU

Photoset by Wilmaset Ltd, Wirral
Printed in England by Clays Ltd, St Ives plc

A CIP record for this book
is available from the British Library

ISBN 0–571–17826–X

2 4 6 8 10 9 7 5 3 1

Translator's Note

It was in no spirit of hubris that I agreed to translate *Eleutheria*. It was rather with a feeling of apprehension. Who am *I* – who is *anyone* – to claim to be able to translate Beckett? We all know how he suffered in translating his own work, and that the only reason he did so was that he couldn't accept other people's even most dedicated efforts. And *Eleutheria* is a play he refused to translate himself, and said he wanted to jettison.

Recently, Les Éditions de Minuit decided that there were imperative reasons for publishing the play in French,* and Faber decided that the same reasons applied to the production of an English translation. Before involving myself, I read *Eleutheria* two or three or four times. With each reading I liked the play more, saw more in it, and in the end I couldn't help feeling that Beckett was mistaken in wishing to suppress it as unworthy of him. Of course it is different from his other works, but that may even add to its interest; he was writing it at the same time as he wrote *Godot* – 1947. To me, it gives no impression of a relative novice feeling his way, and although it is as different from *Godot* as is, say, *Godot* from *Rockaby*, it is still true to Beckett, true to his philosophy – and it is also very funny.

Of his translation of *Fin de Partie*, Beckett wrote to Thomas McGreevy: 'Sick and tired I am of translation and what a losing battle it is always.' And to Alan Schneider: 'It will inevitably be a poor substitute for the

*For an account of the circumstances leading to this decision interested readers are referred to the Preface to the original French text published by Les Éditions de Minuit.

original.' Yet it seemed that some sort of a substitute for the original of *Eleutheria* had to be made for the Anglo-Saxon public. Discussion with friends and colleagues reinforced my conviction that I should try to retain the French atmosphere as much as possible, which is what Beckett did in his translation of *Godot*.

I studied all Beckett's self-translations, and decided that I must never use a word that he would not have used. On the other hand it was out of the question to try to imitate him. I was tempted, for a time, on the very first page of *Eleutheria*, to write: 'Immobility of Madame Krap', and 'Incomprehension of Jacques' – a formulation Beckett often uses, as, for instance, 'Impatience of Willie's fingers'. And of course, every translator is always infinitely envious of the self-translator, who has total liberty to change anything he feels like changing, if it sounds better in the language he is translating into. Working with Patrick Bowles on the translation of *Molloy*, Beckett told Bowles: 'You wouldn't say that in English, you'd say something else.' And Richard Seaver, who worked with him on *La Fin*, wrote: 'I could not have taken the liberties that he did.'

And nor could anyone. A few years ago, Steven Connor gave a talk at Birkbeck College entitled 'Beckett's Self-Translation', and some of the examples he gave were enlightening – and maybe even challenging. From *Mercier et Camier*, for instance: 'la petite voix implorante . . . qui nous parle parfois de vies antérieures' – 'the faint imploring voice . . . that drivels to us on and off of former lives'. Even though we all know that in practice – and even in theory – a translator must be free to stray from word-for-word fidelity in order to achieve the greater fidelity of tone, feeling, rhythm . . . who else would have felt confident enough to insert that marvellous word 'drivels'?

Barbara Wright

ELEUTHERIA

Characters

M. Henri Krap
Mme Henri Krap
Victor Krap, their son
Mme Meck, friend of the Kraps
Dr André Piouk
Mme André Piouk, Mme Krap's sister
Mlle Olga Skunk, Victor's fiancée
A glazier
Michel, his son
A spectator
Chouchi, Chinese torturer
Mme Karl, Victor's landlady
Jacques, the Kraps' manservant
Marie, the Kraps' maid, Jacques' fiancée
Thomas, Mme Meck's chauffeur
Joseph, hatchet man
Prompter

PLACE: Paris
TIME: Three consecutive winter afternoons

3

Set

The first two Acts of this play consist of a split set, with two very different décors juxtaposed. Hence there are two simultaneous actions: the main action and the marginal action. The latter is silent, apart from a few short phrases, the stage business there being confined to the vague attitudes and movements of a single character. In fact it is not so much a place of action as a site, which is often empty.

The text is exclusively concerned with the main action. The marginal action is for the actor to determine, within the limits of the indications in the following note.

Note on the layout of the stage and the marginal action

In the first two acts, the stage represents two different rooms, which are supposed to be in two different places, although here juxtaposed without a dividing wall. The one is Victor's room, the other a corner of the small salon in his parents' flat: it is as if the latter is an enclave of the former. Victor's room moves imperceptibly into the Kraps' salon, as the dirty into the clean, the sordid into the respectable, emptiness into clutter. The two rooms share the whole width of the rear wall as well as the same floor, but when they pass from Victor to his family they become domesticated and respectable. Like the water from the open sea becoming the water in the harbour. The theatrical effect of this dualist space, then, should be produced less by the transition than by the fact that Victor's room takes up three quarters of the stage, and by the flagrant discrepancy between the furniture on either side. In

Victor's room there is nothing but a folding bed; in the Kraps' salon, a very elegant round table, four period chairs, an armchair, a floor lamp and a wall lamp.

The lighting during the day is the same on both sides (window in the centre of the rear wall). But each has its own artificial lighting: for Victor (Acts II and III), the bulb provided by the glazier; for the Kraps' salon (Acts I and II), the floor lamp, and, at the end of the first act, the wall lamp, which stays on after the floor lamp has been switched off.

Each side has its own door.

Victor's room is seen from a different angle in each act; in the first act it is, to the audience, left of the Krap enclave, and in the second act, to their right. Hence, in both acts the main action remains on the right. This also explains why there is no marginal action in the third act, as the Krap side has fallen into the orchestra pit during the change of scene.

The main action and the marginal action never encroach on each other, and barely comment one on the other. The movements of the characters towards each other are brought to a halt by the barrier, which only they can see. This doesn't prevent them almost touching one another at moments. The marginal action in the first two acts must always be as unobtrusive as possible. Most of the time it is only a question of a site and of a person in stasis. The rare functionally necessary movements, such as Mme Karl's entry and Victor's exit in the first act, and Victor's entry and exit in the second, and the two phrases (that of Mme Karl in the first act and of Jacques in the second) should be marked by a kind of hesitancy in the main action, which anyway is often hesitant.

In the first act, the marginal action takes place in Victor's room; in the second, in the Kraps' salon.

Marginal action, Act I

Victor on his bed. Motionless. The audience do not necessarily see him at first. He becomes restless, sits on the bed, stands up, paces up and down in his socks in all directions, from the window to the footlights, from the door to the invisible barrier between him and the main action, slowly and vaguely, keeps stopping, looks out of the window, looks at the audience, goes back and sits on the bed, lies down again, becomes motionless, stands up, starts pacing again, etc. But most of the time he stays where he is, either motionless or restless. His movements, although vague, nevertheless follow a fixed rhythm and pattern, so that the audience finally become more or less aware of where he is without having to look at him.

At one point, that's to say as soon as Mme Krap has had time to arrive, Mme Karl enters and says, 'Your mother.' Victor is sitting on the bed. Silence. He stands up, looks for something (his shoes), doesn't find them, goes out in his socks. The room is empty. Gradually getting darker. Victor returns after, say, five minutes, carries on as before. He must be lying down and motionless during the whole of the end of the main action, the scene between M. Krap and Jacques.

Marginal action, Act II

Stage empty for a long time. Enter Jacques. He walks up and down, exits. Stage again empty for a long time. Enter Jacques. He walks up and down, exits. The audience can sense that he is thinking about his master, whose armchair he gently touches several times. Stage again empty. Enter Jacques. He switches on the floor lamp, walks up and down, exits. Stage again empty. At one moment, that's to say as soon as Victor has had time to arrive, Jacques shows him in. Victor sits down in his father's armchair under the

7

floor lamp. He remains motionless for a long time. Enter Jacques. 'If monsieur will come this way.' Victor stands up and exits. Stage empty until the end of the act.

Act I

A corner of the Kraps' small salon.
   *Round table, four period chairs, club armchair, floor
lamp, wall lamp with shade.*
   Late afternoon, winter.
   Mme Krap sitting at the table.
   Mme Krap motionless.

   A knock. Silence. Another knock.

Mme Krap (*with a start*) Come in.

   *Enter Jacques. He holds a tray out to Mme Krap; it has a
visiting card on it. She takes the card, looks at it, puts it
back on the tray.*

Well?

   Jacques doesn't understand.

Well?

   Jacques doesn't understand.

What an idiot!

   Jacques hangs his head.

I thought I told you that I wasn't at home to anyone but
Madame Meck.

Jacques Yes, madame, but it is madame's sister, madame,
so I thought . . .

Mme Krap My sister!

Jacques Yes, madame.

Mme Krap Impertinent fellow.

Jacques hangs his head.

Show me that card.

Jacques holds out the tray again. Mme Krap takes the card again.

Since when has my sister been called Madame Piouk?

Jacques (*embarrassed*) I think . . .

Mme Krap You think?

Jacques If madame were to reverse the card.

Mme Krap reverses the card and reads.

Mme Krap Couldn't you have told me straightaway?

Jacques If madame will be so good as to excuse me . . .

Mme Krap Don't be so humble.

Jacques remains silent.

Think about your union.

Jacques Madame must be joking.

Mme Krap Show her in.

Jacques starts to go out.

Send me Marie.

Jacques Very good, madame.

Exit. Mme Krap motionless. Enter Jacques.

Madame Piouk.

Enter Mme Piouk hurriedly. Exit Jacques.

Mme Piouk Violette!

Mme Krap Marguerite!

They kiss.

Mme Piouk Violette!

Mme Krap Forgive me if I don't get up. I have a slight pain in . . . oh, it doesn't matter. Sit down. I thought you were in Rome.

Mme Piouk (*sitting down*) You look dreadful!

Mme Krap You don't look very flourishing yourself.

Mme Piouk It's the journey.

Mme Krap Who is this (*looking at the card*), this Piouk?

Mme Piouk He's a doctor.

Mme Krap I didn't ask you what he does.

A knock.

Come in.

Enter Marie.

You can bring the tea.

Marie Very good, madame. (*She starts to go out.*)

Mme Piouk Not for me.

Mme Krap Marie!

Marie Madame?

Mme Krap You can bring the tea when madame Meck gets here.

Marie Very good, madame. (*Exit.*)

Mme Piouk Aren't you going to offer me anything else?

Mme Krap Such as what?

11

Mme Piouk Some port.

Mme Krap It's tea-time.

Mme Piouk How is Henri?

Mme Krap Not well.

Mme Piouk What's the matter with him?

Mme Krap I don't know, he can't urinate.

Mme Piouk It's his prostate.

Mme Krap So you're married?

Mme Piouk Yes.

Mme Krap At your age!

Mme Piouk We love each other.

Mme Krap What's that got to do with it?

Mme Piouk remains silent.

But you must . . . I mean . . . you must be past the . . . the thing is . . . let's think . . .

Mme Piouk Not yet.

Mme Krap Congratulations.

Mme Piouk He wants a child.

Mme Krap No!

Mme Piouk Yes!

Mme Krap That's madness.

Mme Piouk How's Victor?

Mme Krap Still the same, still there, in that dump of his. We never see him. (*pause*) Let's not talk about him.

Mme Piouk You're expecting Madame Meck?

Mme Krap Not very eagerly.

Mme Piouk That old witch.

Mme Krap Don't you want to see her?

Mme Piouk I'd just as soon not.

Mme Krap She likes you, though.

Mme Piouk You're joking! It's all put on.

Mme Krap Yes, probably. (*pause*) I'm expecting her at any minute.

Mme Piouk I'll go, then. (*She stands up.*)

Mme Krap Didn't your husband come with you?

Mme Piouk (*sitting down again*) Ah, I can't wait for you to see him! He's so kind, so intelligent, so . . .

Mme Krap Didn't he come with you?

Mme Piouk He went to the hotel.

Mme Krap Which hotel?

Mme Piouk I don't know.

Mme Krap When will you know?

Mme Piouk He was to come and fetch me here.

Mme Krap When?

Mme Piouk Oh, in about half an hour, I think.

Mme Krap Then you can't go.

Mme Piouk I was going to wait for him in the large salon.

Mme Krap What sort of medicine does he practise?

Mme Piouk He has no speciality. That's to say . . .

Mme Krap He does everything.

Mme Piouk He is especially interested in humanity.

Mme Krap Where does he hold sway?

Mme Piouk He's hoping to set up here.

Mme Krap And until now?

Mme Piouk All over the place.

Mme Krap I haven't congratulated you yet.

She sticks a cheek out, and Mme Piouk kisses it.

You might have let me know.

Mme Piouk I wanted to send you a telegram, but André said . . .

Mme Krap Ah well, it's of no importance.

A knock.

Come in.

Enter Jacques.

Jacques Madame Meck.

Enter Mme Meck, a voluminous woman, heavily laden with furs, cloaks, umbrella, handbag, etc. Exit Jacques.

Mme Meck Violette!

Mme Krap Jeanne!

They kiss. Mme Meck sits down, unburdens herself and arranges her attire.

Forgive me for not getting up.

Mme Meck Are you still in pain?

Mme Krap Worse and worse. You know my sister?

Mme Meck (*turning to Mme Piouk*) Why, it's Rose!

Mme Krap No no, it's Marguerite.

Mme Meck My dear Marguerite!

Holds out her hand. Mme Piouk takes it.

Where have you sprung from? I thought you were in Pisa.

Mme Krap She's married.

Mme Meck Married!

Mme Krap To a doctor who is interested in humanity.

Mme Meck Let me kiss you.

Mme Piouk lets herself be kissed.

Married! Oh! (*making an indescribable movement*) I'm so pleased!

Mme Piouk Thank you.

Mme Meck What's his name?

Mme Krap (*looking at the card*) Piouk. André.

Mme Meck (*ecstatically*) Madame André Piouk!

A knock.

Mme Krap Come in.

Enter Marie with the tea tray. She puts it down on the table.

Is monsieur back?

Marie No, madame.

Mme Krap Send me Jacques.

Marie Very good, madame. (*Exit.*)

Mme Piouk (*to Mme Meck*) My sister doesn't look very well, does she?

Mme Meck Doesn't look very well?

Mme Krap pours out the tea and offers a cup to her sister, who refuses it.

Mme Krap She prefers port.

Mme Meck Port! At five o'clock!

Mme Krap She's right. I'm worn out.

Mme Meck What's wrong?

A knock.

Mme Krap Come in.

Enter Jacques.

Ah, Jacques.

Jacques Madame.

Mme Krap Is monsieur back?

Jacques Not yet, madame.

Mme Krap The moment he comes in, tell him I want to speak to him.

Jacques Very good, madame.

Mme Krap And you can switch the light on.

Jacques Very good, madame. (*He switches on the floor lamp.*)

Mme Krap And the other one.

Jacques Very good, madame. (*He switches on the wall lamp.*)

Mme Krap That's all.

Jacques Very good, madame. (*Exit.*)

Mme Meck How is he?

Mme Krap Who?

Mme Meck Henri.

Mme Krap Not well.

Mme Meck Oh.

Mme Krap He can't pee any more.

Mme Piouk It's his prostate.

Mme Meck Poor man. And him so cheerful, so . . .

Mme Krap And then, he's worried sick.

Mme Meck He's bound to be.

Mme Krap Because of Victor.

Mme Meck Incidentally, how is he?

Mme Krap Who?

Mme Meck Your Victor.

Mme Krap Let's not talk about him.

Mme Meck I'm not very well, either.

Mme Piouk What's the matter with you?

Mme Meck It's my womb. It seems it's becoming prolapsed.

Mme Krap Like mine. Except that mine already *is* prolapsed.

Mme Piouk Isn't there anything to drink in this house?

Mme Krap To drink?

Mme Meck In the middle of the afternoon!

Mme Piouk Henri can't pee any more. Victor we mustn't talk about, and you've got a prolapsing womb.

Mme Krap And you've got married.

Mme Meck Is that any reason to drink?

Mme Krap It doesn't do you any good.

Mme Meck Our little Victor! What a business! And him so cheerful, so lively!

Mme Krap He was never either cheerful or lively.

Mme Meck What! But he was the life and soul of the family for years and years.

Mme Krap The life and soul of the family! Some bargain!

Mme Piouk Is he still living in that cul-de-sac – l'Impasse de l'Enfant-Jésus?

Mme Krap Jeanne sees life and gaiety everywhere. It's a permanent hallucination.

Mme Piouk Is he still living in the Impasse de l'Enfant-Jésus?

Mme Krap Yes.

Mme Piouk He needs shaking out of it.

Mme Krap He doesn't even get out of bed these days. Another cup?

Mme Meck Half a cup. He doesn't even get out of bed, you say?

Mme Piouk He's ill.

Mme Krap There's absolutely nothing the matter with him.

Mme Meck Then why doesn't he get out of bed?

Mme Krap He goes out from time to time.

Mme Meck Then he must get out of bed from time to time.

Mme Krap It's when he has nothing left to eat. Then he rummages through dustbins. He goes as far as Passy. The concierge has seen him.

Mme Meck Fancy! Dustbins in Passy!

Mme Piouk How dreadful.

Mme Krap Yes, isn't it?

Mme Piouk But you do give him money?

Mme Krap Every month. I take it myself.

Mme Piouk And what does he do with it?

Mme Krap I've no idea. It probably isn't enough.

Enter M. Henri Krap.

M. Krap Good evening, Jeanne. Ah, Marguerite. (*They kiss.*) I thought you were in Venice.

Mme Krap Your wife is also present.

M. Krap kisses his wife.

She's married.

Mme Meck To a doctor.

Mme Krap Who loves humanity.

M. Krap (*sadly*) Congratulations.

Mme Krap Sit down.

M. Krap Oh, I'm not staying.

Mme Krap Oh yes you are.

M. Krap You think so? (*Sits down painfully in the armchair.*) I shouldn't. (*Settles back.*) I shan't be able to get up again.

Mme Krap Don't talk nonsense.

M. Krap My freedom diminishes daily. Soon I shan't be allowed to open my mouth. And to think that I counted on talking bullshit until I was at death's door.

Mme Meck What's the matter with him?

Mme Krap He relieves himself as best he can.

M. Krap Yes, I understand that now, now that it's too late. *Nimis sero, imber serotinus.* Peace is peculiar to slaves.

   Pause. Mme Meck grimaces.

I am the cow who arrives at the gate of the slaughterhouse and only then understands all the absurdity of the pastures. She would have done better to think about it earlier, there in the soft tall grass. Never mind. She still has the courtyard to cross. Nobody can take that away from her.

Mme Krap Take no notice. He thinks he's with his circle of friends.

M. Krap I *am* in a circle. The ninth. (*Changing his tone:*) Well well, Marguerite, so you've become a respectable woman.

Mme Piouk Flatterer!

M. Krap Congratulations.

Mme Krap You've already congratulated her.

M. Krap So I have.

Mme Piouk Henri.

M. Krap Yes.

Mme Piouk I'd like something to drink.

M. Krap Of course. (*to Mme Krap:*) Ring the bell.

Mme Krap You know very well I can't get up.

M. Krap Nor you can. Although there's no point. He'll come anyway.

Mme Krap Don't be too sure. He's left us in peace for at least three minutes.

M. Krap Well then, Marguerite, if you'd be kind enough to ring the bell.

Mme Piouk stands up, rings the bell, sits down again.

Mme Krap Yesterday he let a good quarter of an hour go by without sticking his nose in. I thought he was dead.

A knock.

Come in.

Enter Jacques.

M. Krap I wonder why he always knocks. That's fifteen years he's been knocking and we've been telling him to come in, but he goes on knocking.

Mme Meck It's a question of etiquette.

M. Krap (*to Mme Piouk*) What would you like?

Mme Piouk Anything. Some port.

M. Krap (*to Jacques*) Some port.

Jacques Very good, monsieur. (*Exit.*)

Silence.

Mme Piouk We were talking about Victor.

M. Krap Ah.

Mme Krap Is there any other subject of conversation? I'm beginning to wonder.

Mme Meck The poor thing!

Mme Krap (*violently*) Hold your tongue!

Mme Piouk Violette!

Mme Meck What's the matter with her?

Mme Krap I'm sick and tired of people feeling sorry for that monster, it's been going on for two years!

Mme Piouk Monster!

Mme Meck Your own child!

M. Krap Already two years! Only two years!

Mme Krap (*almost hysterical*) Why doesn't he leave the district, the town, the department, the country, why doesn't he go and drop dead . . . in the Balkans!

A knock.

Personally, I . . .

Mme Piouk Come in.

Enter Jacques.

M. Krap What do you want?

Jacques Monsieur rang?

M. Krap No no. The port.

Jacques At once, monsieur. (*Exit.*)

Silence.

Mme Meck You were saying?

Mme Krap I wash my hands of him. (*She stands up painfully.*) I've had enough. (*Walks painfully to the door.*) Enough. (*Exit.*)

Mme Piouk So that's how she can't get up.

Mme Meck Where is she going?

M. Krap (*with a sigh*) To the lavatory, probably. She goes there from time to time.

   Silence.

Mme Meck You look superb.

Mme Piouk She's not serious.

Mme Meck What?

Mme Piouk Violette. It's just words.

Mme Meck Of course. Wash her hands of him indeed! Her only child! Can you imagine!

   A knock.

M. Krap (*not loudly enough*) Come in.

Mme Meck A mother! Saying that!

   Another knock.

Mme Piouk Come in!

   Enter Jacques, carrying a tray. He looks round, wondering where to put it.

Put it on the chair.

   He puts the tray on Mme Krap's chair.

On the other one!

   He puts it on the other one.

Tell Marie to come and clear the table.

23

Jacques Very good, madame. (*Exit.*)

Mme Piouk When you have servants, it doesn't really feel like home any more.

Mme Meck You need them, though.

Silence.

Mme Piouk It's so long since I had any news. *Is* there anything new in this business?

M. Krap What business?

Mme Piouk The Victor business.

M. Krap No new element.

Mme Meck They say he goes as far as the Rue Spontini when he's rummaging through dustbins.

M. Krap Nobody told me.

Mme Piouk You don't seem to care.

M. Krap Don't I?

Mme Meck I've never understood the first thing about this business.

M. Krap From the dramatic point of view, there's no point in my wife's absence.

Mmes Piouk and Meck look at each other. A knock.

Mme Piouk Oh, come in!

Enter Marie. Business with the trays. Exit Marie.

Would you like some?

Mme Meck Just a drop.

Mme Piouk And you, Henri?

M. Krap Uh-uh. Thanks.

Mme Piouk pours port for Mme Meck.

Mme Meck Oh, that's too much! I shall be tiddly! (*She drinks.*) It's strong!

Mme Piouk helps herself, empties her glass in one gulp, pours herself a second.

She's taking a long time.

Mme Piouk What?

Mme Meck Violette is taking a long time.

M. Krap You think so?

Mme Piouk But something must be done! We can't leave him like that.

M. Krap Like what?

Mme Piouk In that state of . . . of sordid inertia.

M. Krap Since that's what he wants.

Mme Piouk But it's a disgrace to the family!

Mme Meck He's too old to behave like that.

Mme Piouk It'll kill Violette.

M. Krap You don't know her.

Silence.

Mme Piouk (*to Mme Meck*) How is the general?

Silence.

Or should I say: the field-marshal?

Handkerchief of Mme Meck.

M. Krap Really, Marguerite, do think before you speak.

Mme Piouk I don't understand.

M. Krap There's a slight difference between mourning and elegance.

Mme Piouk Oh, my poor Jeanne, I didn't know, I'm so sorry, forgive me, please forgive me.

Mme Meck (*drawing on the military tradition*) His dying breath was for France.

A knock.

Mme Piouk This is becoming impossible.

M. Krap We'd do better to leave the door open. Or get rid of it altogether.

Another knock.

Mme Piouk Oh, come in for goodness' sake!

Enter Jacques.

Jacques Doctor Piouk.

M. Krap Never heard of him.

Mme Piouk André! (*She rushes out.*)

M. Krap Who?

Mme Meck Her husband.

M. Krap (*to Jacques*) Have you seen madame?

Jacques Madame has gone out, monsieur.

M. Krap Gone out!

Jacques Yes, monsieur.

M. Krap On foot?

Jacques Yes, monsieur.

M. Krap She didn't say where she was going?

Jacques Madame didn't say anything, monsieur.

M. Krap That'll do.

Exit Jacques.

Mme Meck 'Long live France!' Then he entered into a coma.

M. Krap I beg your pardon?

Mme Meck I was reliving Ludovic's last moments.

M. Krap And then?

Mme Meck He suddenly sat bolt upright, and cried out: 'Long live France!' Then he fell back, and the death rattle began.

M. Krap He was able to sit bolt upright?

Mme Meck Yes, to the great astonishment of us all.

Enter Mme and Dr Piouk. He is a hideous man. Introductions. Embarrassed silence. Dr Piouk sits down.

Mme Piouk A little port, dearest?

Dr Piouk Uh-uh. Thanks.

Mme Piouk Uh-uh no or uh-uh yes?

Dr Piouk Uh-uh no. Thanks.

M. Krap Forgive me if I don't get up. I have a slight pain in . . . I'm tired.

Dr Piouk Are you ill?

M. Krap I'm dying.

Mme Meck Really, Henri, do calm down.

M. Krap And I certainly don't expect to astonish anyone . . .

Mme Meck Henri!

M. Krap . . . when I sit bolt upright . . .

Mme Piouk Where is Violette?

M. Krap . . . and they see I've shot my bolt. Ha ha!

Dr Piouk A little port, after all.

Mme Piouk pours it for him.

Mme Meck She's gone out.

M. Krap What?

Mme Meck Marguerite asked where Violette is. I told her she's gone out.

Mme Piouk (*decanter in hand*) Gone out!

M. Krap On foot.

Mme Meck Without saying where she was going.

M. Krap She'll be back before long.

Mme Piouk Did she tell you so?

M. Krap She's always back before long.

Mme Meck I sincerely hope you're right.

M. Krap Why?

Mme Meck I shall be able to leave easy in my mind . . .

M. Krap My son is in the right.

Mme Piouk Henri!

M. Krap I've loosed my chains.

Mme Meck (*pursuing her thought*) . . . without imagining her covered in blood, knocked over by a lorry.

M. Krap She's the one who knocks lorries over.

Dr Piouk (*standing up*) Darling . . .

M. Krap Dearest, darling . . .

Dr Piouk It's time for us to go.

M. Krap Jeanne.

Mme Meck Henri?

M. Krap Do you remember when Violette and I were first married?

Mme Meck Do I remember!

M. Krap Before we learnt to appreciate each other.

Mme Meck Ah! The good old days!

M. Krap Did I ever call her darling?

Mme Meck You used to bill and coo.

M. Krap It's unimaginable.

Dr Piouk (*still standing*) Marguerite.

Mme Piouk I'm coming, dearest.

M. Krap My wife will be so sorry. Most upset.

Mme Meck I ought to be going, too.

M. Krap But you're staying.

Mme Meck Well, er . . .

M. Krap You see, the outside world is calling her, but she resists the temptation. Whereas Marguerite has never done anything she didn't want to do. I'm not getting at you, Doctor.

Mme Meck You are very disagreeable, Henri.

M. Krap (*without enthusiasm*) Stay to dinner, we're having a cold meal.

Dr Piouk Too kind. Unfortunately we have an engagement.

M. Krap (*ribaldly, to Mme Meck*) What a hurry they're in!

Mme Meck Wait another five minutes.

M. Krap Let's have a little continence, eh.

Mme Meck I'll give you a lift. In the Delage.

Dr Piouk Well, Marguerite?

Mme Piouk Whatever you like, dearest.

M. Krap The longer you wait, the better it is.

Mme Piouk I so wanted you to . . . Violette to know you.

Dr Piouk sits down again. Silence.

M. Krap Have a cigar.

Dr Piouk Uh-uh. Thanks.

M. Krap Uh-uh no or uh-uh yes?

Dr Piouk I don't smoke.

Silence.

Mme Meck }
Mme Piouk } (*together*) I . . .

Mme Meck Oh, sorry. You were going to say?

Mme Piouk Oh, nothing. Carry on.

Silence.

M. Krap Come on, Jeanne, out with it.

Mme Meck (*after some thought*) My goodness, I don't remember.

Silence.

M. Krap Being incapable of thought myself, my internal organs have taken over that task.

Silence.

You are the person, Doctor, with whom I am doing my best to communicate.

Dr Piouk Oh, you know, I'm not much of a conversationalist.

Mme Piouk He does so much thinking!

M. Krap And yet, what I have just said is not devoid of intelligence.

Dr Piouk It's nonsense.

M. Krap Well well! In what sense?

Dr Piouk You *are* your organs, monsieur, and your organs are you.

M. Krap I am my organs?

Dr Piouk Precisely.

M. Krap You frighten me.

Mme Meck (*scenting a free consultation*) And I, Doctor, am I my organs, too?

Dr Piouk Without the slightest residue, madame.

M. Krap What a pleasure it is to meet an intelligent man at last!

Mme Piouk (*ecstatically*) André!

M. Krap Do go on. Develop that grandiose thought.

Dr Piouk This isn't the moment.

M. Krap Before that mass of worn-out organs, my wife, comes back.

Mme Piouk Henri!

Dr Piouk For heaven's sake!

M. Krap I'm going to have to consult you.

A knock.

Mme Piouk Come in.

Enter Jacques.

Jacques Mademoiselle Skunk.

Enter Mlle Skunk, an alluring young lady. Greetings; hers are sullen. Exit Jacques.

Mme Piouk Do you remember me?

Mlle Skunk Of course.

Mme Piouk It was in Évian, two years ago.

Mlle Skunk What was I doing there?

Silence.

Mme Piouk May I introduce my husband, Doctor Piouk.

Mlle Skunk sits down in Mme Krap's place.

Mme Meck You look superb.

Mme Piouk A little port?

Mlle Skunk If you like.

M. Krap Doctor.

Dr Piouk (*jerked out of his thoughts, with an ostentatious start*) Did someone call me?

M. Krap I'm wondering what you are going to contribute to this comedy.

Dr Piouk (*after mature reflection*) I hope I may be of some use.

Mme Meck (*worried*) I don't understand.

Dr Piouk And you, dear monsieur, is your role well delineated?

M. Krap It's eliminated.

Dr Piouk But you're still on stage.

M. Krap So it would seem.

Mme Meck I absolutely must go.

M. Krap Go then, my dear Jeanne, go, since you absolutely must. We don't need you.

Mlle Skunk Where is Violette?

Dr Piouk (*to M. Krap*) If you make a little effort, you might manage to keep the punters amused.

M. Krap Do you really think so? Honestly?

Dr Piouk I say what I think.

M. Krap I hadn't imagined that possibility.

Mlle Skunk Where is Violette?

Mme Meck This is becoming worrying.

M. Krap What did you say?

Mme Meck Olga asked where Violette is, and I said this is becoming worrying.

M. Krap What is becoming worrying?

Mme Meck Her disproportionate absence.

M. Krap Her disproportionate absence! No one but Jeanne could talk like that.

Mlle Skunk Where did she go?

Mme Meck We don't know.

M. Krap On goodness knows what sudden impulse, she left the house, on foot. For a long time we thought she was in the lavatory. That's right, Doctor?

Dr Piouk Too subtle. Persevere.

Mlle Skunk She asked me to call before dinner.

M. Krap She wanted to speak to you?

Mlle Skunk Yes, about things that couldn't wait.

M. Krap Me too, she wanted to speak to me, so it seems. And, anyway, that's the only reason why I'm here with you, as you can well imagine. But she hasn't said anything to me yet.

Mme Meck (*to Mlle Skunk*) Have you seen Victor?

M. Krap And now *I'm* going to speak to *her*.

Mlle Skunk Last week.

M. Krap (*to Dr Piouk*) Mlle Skunk is my son's fiancée.

Dr Piouk Fortunate young man.

Mlle Skunk (*bitterly*) He's beside himself with joy.

  Dr Piouk lights a cigarette.

M. Krap I thought you didn't smoke.

Dr Piouk I lied.

Mme Meck I really will have to go.

M. Krap Don't start again.

Mme Meck What are we going to do?

M. Krap The time we waste with these people! Go, then. We'll phone you.

Mlle Skunk I'll come with you.

A strident voice is heard.

M. Krap Yoo-hoo. Here she is.

Mme Meck At last!

Dr Piouk (*to Mlle Skunk*) Are you French, mademoiselle?

Mlle Skunk No, monsieur.

Mme Meck Are you sure that's her?

M. Krap I am perfectly certain.

Dr Piouk Scandinavian?

A knock.

Mme Piouk Come in.

Enter Jacques.

Jacques Madame requests monsieur . . .

M. Krap That sounds like a classified ad.

Mme Meck Is madame all right?

M. Krap Tell madame that . . . (*Changes his mind.*) Help me to resuscitate.

Jacques hurries over, helps M. Krap up, wants to assist him to the door. M. Krap waves him away. At the door, he turns round.

You see: once I'm on my feet I can walk by myself! I'm going out!

He goes out. He comes in again.

I'm coming in again! And I'm going out again!

He goes out again, followed by Jacques.

Mme Meck Henri has changed a lot.

Dr Piouk Don't tell me you're English.

Mme Meck He thinks he's condemned, so he no longer controls himself.

Mme Piouk Very convenient.

Dr Piouk (*discouraged*) He's a remarkable man.

Mme Piouk Do you really think so?

Dr Piouk I say what I think.

Mme Piouk But from what point of view?

Dr Piouk It's hard to say.

Mme Piouk It's certainly the first time I've heard that.

Dr Piouk What does he do?

Mme Meck (*proudly*) He's a man of letters.

Dr Piouk Well well!

Enter M. Krap. He reaches his chair and sits down cautiously.

M. Krap You were saying something nice about me, I can feel it.

Mme Meck Is she all right?

M. Krap She is unscathed.

Mme Meck Is she coming in?

M. Krap She is about to do so.

Mme Piouk In the old days, you were natural.

M. Krap At the cost of what artifices!

Dr Piouk You are a writer, monsieur?

M. Krap (*indignant*) What right have you . . .

Dr Piouk One can sense it from the way you express yourself.

Mme Piouk Where has she been?

Mme Meck She'll tell us.

M. Krap I'll be frank with you. I *was* a writer.

Mme Meck He's a Member of the Institute!

M. Krap You see.

Dr Piouk What genre?

M. Krap I don't follow you.

Dr Piouk I was referring to your writings. For what literary genre did you have a preference?

M. Krap The shit genre.

Mme Piouk Really?

Dr Piouk In prose or in verse?

M. Krap One day the one, another day the other.

Dr Piouk And you now consider your work complete?

M. Krap The God has spat me out.

Dr Piouk Doesn't a little book of memoirs tempt you?

M. Krap That would spoil my death throes.

Mme Meck You must agree that this is a strange way to treat one's guests.

Mlle Skunk Extremely curious.

M. Krap Marguerite, would you mind changing places with Olga?

Mme Piouk I'm quite comfortable where I am.

M. Krap I know. We're all quite comfortable where we are. Very, very comfortable. Unfortunately, it isn't a question of our comfort.

Mme Meck What is this latest bee in his bonnet?

M. Krap You see, Marguerite, since you insist on knowing everything, whether you are seen or not seen is, as it were, of no importance. If you were to disappear at this very moment, I personally would not have the slightest objection. Olga, on the other hand, has a place among us only in so far as she displays her charms, by which I mean her bosom and her legs, because her face is rather commonplace.

Mme Piouk My congratulations; you're more of a boor than ever.

M. Krap You've no reason to take offence, Marguerite. As a brother-in-law I am very, very fond of you, and I should be absolutely devastated if you were to leave us. But as a . . . how shall I put it . . . (*He snaps his fingers.*)

Dr Piouk Hierophant.

M. Krap If you like.

  Silence.

Dr Piouk Finish your sentence, though.

M. Krap What was I saying?

Dr Piouk Brother-in-law, you're fond of her; hierophant, you . . . ?

M. Krap (*in a broken voice*) I have no family.

38

Mme Piouk He's crying!

Dr Piouk Do what he asks you, Marguerite.

Mme Piouk and Mlle Skunk change places.

M. Krap (*to Mlle Skunk*) Open your jacket. Cross your legs. Pull up your skirt. (*He helps her.*) There. Now don't move.

Dr Piouk It's what we call a temporary aberration.

M. Krap I am rather subject to them.

Mme Meck (*flaring up*) I've had enough!

M. Krap We've all had enough. But that's not the point.

Mme Meck For me it is the point. (*Stands up massively and gathers together her numerous belongings. Rummages in her enormous handbag, finally brings out a card and reads.*) 'I must see you. Come to tea tomorrow. I have thousands of things to tell you. We shall be on our own.' (*She leaves time for this message to take effect.*) I don't like people making a fool of me.

M. Krap People really are extraordinary.

Dr Piouk It's human nature.

M. Krap So long as they don't think you're making a fool of them, they'll put up with anything.

Dr Piouk That's the way we're made.

M. Krap You'd do better to sit down again, my poor Jeanne, rather than shilly-shally on your feet, with all your equipment weighing you down. She's upstaging everyone, my goodness! Although she has no part to play in this scene.

Mme Meck (*in the tones of a prophetess*) I'm only an ugly old woman, ill and alone. Yet the time will come when you will all envy me.

Silence.

M. Krap So there!

Exit Mme Meck, slamming the door.

Dr Piouk She's far-sighted.

M. Krap But whom do we not envy?

Dr Piouk She may well have a function that you don't suspect.

M. Krap You're getting caught up in this game, Doctor. Watch out!

Dr Piouk I don't deny its appeal.

Mlle Skunk (*yawning profoundly*) Excuse me!

Mme Piouk How horrible this light is!

Mlle Skunk You aren't in it any more, though.

Mme Piouk No, but now I can see it.

Mlle Skunk What's this barbed wire for? (*She points to a thin strip of barbed wire fixed under the edge of the table and running down to the floor.*)

Mme Piouk Barbed wire?

Mlle Skunk (*touching it*) It's got spikes! Look!

Mme Piouk stands up and leans over the table.

Mme Piouk How is it that I hadn't noticed it?

Dr Piouk My wife is not very sensitive to the macrocosm.

M. Krap But she reacted to the light.

Dr Piouk That's because she really suffered from it.

Mlle Skunk But what does it mean?

M. Krap That's Victor's place.

Dr Piouk He's your son?

M. Krap Yes, I'm sure of that now.

Dr Piouk Did he take up a lot of space?

M. Krap Yes, he took up a lot of space in this house.

Mlle Skunk I don't understand.

M. Krap What don't you understand, Olga dear?

Mlle Skunk What that (*pointing to the wire*) has to do with Victor.

M. Krap You have to explain everything to them.

Dr Piouk That's the way women are.

M. Krap You see, Olga dear, ever since Victor left, about two years ago, I think . . .

Mlle Skunk Two years! Two years and five months!

M. Krap What does it matter?

Mlle Skunk Even so!

M. Krap Am I to go on?

Silence.

Ever since that . . . er . . . that event, my wife has always wanted to keep – yet in a way abolish – our son's favourite places, for we all, Victor, my wife and I, had our favourite places in this house, as far back as my memory reaches, and personally I still have mine. (*pause*) This plan was put off for a long time but last week, I don't know why, my wife put it into practice, with the result you see. And that's only the beginning. The flat will soon be covered in barbed wire. (*pause*) It must be added, in Violette's defence, that for a whole afternoon she remained under the influence of the Surrealist exhibition. (*pause*) Is that clear enough?

Dr Piouk Much too clear. You've ruined everything.

M. Krap Doctor, you disappoint me.

Dr Piouk Are you insinuating that I have said something stupid?

Mme Piouk He's mad.

M. Krap Something enormously stupid, Doctor. Because we must laugh at our laughter.

Dr Piouk You're right, Marguerite.

Enter Mme Krap.

M. Krap Here's something solid.

Mme Piouk André, this is my sister. Violette, I . . .

Dr Piouk stands up.

M. Krap Forgive me if I don't get up. I have a slight pain in . . .

Mme Krap Marguerite, you've taken my place.

Mme Piouk (*standing up hastily*) Have it.

Mme Krap sits down in her place. Mme Piouk takes Mme Meck's chair.

Mme Krap Good evening, Olga.

Mlle Skunk Good evening. You wanted to see me?

Mme Krap Yes. Who is that man?

Mme Piouk He's my husband. (*She stands up*.) Are you coming, André?

Mme Krap (*vigorously*) Sit down!

Mme Piouk hesitates.

M. Krap Beware!

Mme Piouk sits down again.

Mme Krap Doctor . . . what was it . . .

Dr Piouk Piouk. (*He bows, and sits down again.*)

Mme Krap Marguerite told us that you love humanity. Is that possible?

Mme Piouk You're twisting my words.

Dr Piouk I don't love it.

Mme Piouk He's interested in it. Full stop.

Mme Krap You're interested in humanity?

Dr Piouk I am not indifferent to it.

Mme Krap You wouldn't be a Communist?

Dr Piouk My private life is *my* business.

M. Krap Don't make matters worse, Doctor.

Mme Piouk Where have you been? We were beginning to get worried. André didn't want to wait. But when I told him how much you wanted to meet him . . .

Mme Krap It's a thorny question.

Dr Piouk What is?

Mme Krap The problem of humanity.

Dr Piouk At first sight, yes.

M. Krap The best thinkers have tackled it.

Dr Piouk I make no claim to have surpassed them.

Mme Krap And what is your solution?

Dr Piouk My solution?

M. Krap In two words.

Mme Krap (*severely*) You have one, I hope.

Dr Piouk It lacks charm.

M. Krap Inevitably.

Dr Piouk Is this the right moment?

M. Krap This is certainly the first time that I have heard anyone taking so much persuading . . .

Mme Krap Hold your tongue!

M. Krap . . . to resolve the situation of the human species.

Dr Piouk I think the moment is ill-chosen.

Mme Krap That's our business.

M. Krap Do your duty.

Dr Piouk Well, this is what I would do . . .

M. Krap *Is* there anything to be done?

Dr Piouk I am a practical man.

Mme Krap *Will* you hold your tongue!

M. Krap Yes, Violette, with pleasure.

Mme Krap We're listening.

Dr Piouk Well, then. I would ban reproduction. I would perfect the condom and other devices and bring them into general use. I would establish teams of abortionists, controlled by the State. I would apply the death penalty to any woman guilty of giving birth. I would drown all newborn babies. I would militate in favour of homosexuality, and would myself set the example. And to speed things up, I would encourage recourse to euthanasia by all possible means, although I would not make it obligatory. Those are the broad outlines.

Mme Krap I was born too early.

M. Krap Much too early.

Dr Piouk I make no claim to originality. It's a question of organisation. That is where I have extended the horizons. In two years' time, everything will be finalised. Unfortunately, my forces are in decline. And so are my resources.

Mme Krap What about that child you want?

Dr Piouk Who told you I wanted a child?

Silence.

Mme Piouk (*to Mme Krap*) You are odious.

Mme Krap You'll kill her, Doctor.

Dr Piouk I want a child, *primo*, to entertain me in my leisure hours, which are ever becoming briefer and more desolate; *secundo*, so that he can receive the torch from my hands, when they are no longer strong enough to carry it.

M. Krap That's certainly the advantage of having sons.

Mme Krap But you'll kill her.

Dr Piouk I have debated this question at length with your sister, madame, both before and after our union. Have I not, Marguerite?

Mme Piouk You were perfect.

Dr Piouk In the delightful and terrible weeks that preceded our commitment, while we were wandering, hand in hand, in the Campagna, or were taking counsel from the

45

moon on the terraces at Tivoli, our conversation turned almost entirely on that subject. Did it not, Marguerite?

Mme Piouk Almost exclusively, dearest.

Mme Krap (*to M. Krap*) What's got into you, sniggering to yourself like that?

M. Krap I was thinking of the moon you and I once took counsel from.

Dr Piouk When we were finally engaged, we had some atrocious times. For my part, nothing on earth could induce me to relive them.

M. Krap What can you do, that's the way human fiancés are. I remember one evening, in Robinson, we were climbing up the steps in that chestnut tree, Violette went first, and I assure you . . .

Mme Krap Hold your tongue!

Dr Piouk And since our official, open cohabitation, which, incidentally, was blessed by His Holiness, how many nights have we not spent, until cockcrow, weighing up the pros and cons, incapable of coming to a decision!

M. Krap You should have put your head down and charged.

Dr Piouk That's what we did . . . (*He brings out his pocket diary and flicks through it.*) Just a minute . . . last Saturday night. (*He turns over a few pages, makes a note, returns the diary to his pocket.*) You see, we were tired of finessing. (*expressive gesture*) And now, we're waiting. (*He stands up.*) And come what may.

Mme Krap What's the matter with you?

Dr Piouk The matter with me?

Mme Krap You aren't going to leave us?

M. Krap I did invite them to dinner. But they're dying to be alone.

Mme Krap To stay to dinner? To eat what?

M. Krap I don't know. Yesterday's lamb.

Mme Krap Lamb! Mutton, you mean. What am I saying, mutton, ram, the whole house smelt of wool and copulation.

Dr Piouk You tempt me. Unfortunately, we have an engagement.

M. Krap Put yourself in their place.

Mme Krap If I were fifty years – no, that's too much – forty years younger, Doctor, I would follow you into all the dark corners, even though your actual person has very little effect on me. But when you speak . . . ! (*to M. Krap:*) What did you say?

M. Krap Nothing. I was shuddering.

Mme Piouk They're expecting us.

Dr Piouk Let's not exaggerate, darling.

Mme Krap Let's go to the Terminus.

Dr Piouk Mademoiselle Skunk isn't saying anything.

Mlle Skunk What do you expect me to say? I'm waiting to find out why I was summoned.

Mme Krap You can come with us. We'll all get drunk.

Dr Piouk I adore blow-outs.

M. Krap And what about your womb?

Mme Krap I'll discuss it with the doctor. May I, Doctor?

Dr Piouk Not before the cheese, dear madame.

Mme Krap What a rascal!

Mme Piouk (*to Mme Krap*) Your outing did you good.

Silence.

Dr Piouk Will you come, mademoiselle?

Mlle Skunk I am free.

Mme Krap That's settled, then. At the Terminus, in half an hour.

All stand up, except M. Krap and Mlle Skunk.

Dr Piouk (*to M. Krap*) See you later. I have a great many things to say to you.

M. Krap Forgive me if I don't get up, I have a slight . . .

Mme Krap I'll see you out. Are you going to come, Olga?

Mlle Skunk I'll wait for you. I don't feel like changing.

Dr Piouk (*to Mlle Skunk*) Without fail, hm?

Mme Krap (*to Mlle Skunk*) It's up to you.

Exeunt Mme Krap, Mme and Dr Piouk. Fairly long silence.

M. Krap Open your jacket.

Mlle Skunk I'm cold.

M. Krap That doesn't matter. Pull up your skirt. Further. There. Now, keep still. Breathe.

Mlle Skunk takes her head in her hands, doubles up, and weeps. She is shaken with sobs.

For God's sake!

The crying fit continues.

Stop it!

Mlle Skunk sobs even harder.

She cries like a slattern. (*raising his voice:*) You're ugly, Olga, do you hear me, as ugly as sin. We're buggered.

Mlle Skunk gradually calms down, raises her ravaged face, crosses her legs, which her distress had uncrossed, pulls up her skirt, etc.

You're pretty! Who taught you to snivel like a . . . (*He is loath to repeat himself.*) like a . . . (*He can't find the words.*) like in real life? You're forgetting where you are.

Mlle Skunk You know very well.

M. Krap What?

Mlle Skunk Who taught me.

M. Krap That's not the point. What about me, do you think I don't feel like bawling? Only, I, if I once . . . (*He interrupts himself, suddenly struck by a dreadful suspicion.*) You never let yourself go like that in front of him, at least?

Mlle Skunk Of course not.

M. Krap Honestly?

Mlle Skunk Yes.

M. Krap Then all is not yet lost.

Mlle Skunk I ought to have, probably.

M. Krap What?

Mlle Skunk Cried like that in real life, in front of him.

Silence

M. Krap It wouldn't have done much good.

Mlle Skunk It might have.

Silence.

M. Krap I haven't got much longer.

Mlle Skunk You mustn't say that.

M. Krap I want to unburden myself. (*pause*) For once. (*pause*) To someone who doesn't hate me. (*pause*) But perhaps you do hate me?

Mlle Skunk You know very well I don't.

M. Krap Why not?

Mlle Skunk I don't know.

M. Krap It's something I think I've only recently found out.

Silence.

Will you let me?

Mlle Skunk I'm so stupid.

M. Krap What does that matter?

Mlle Skunk I shan't understand.

M. Krap Will you think about it from time to time?

Mlle Skunk Of course, Father.

M. Krap Father?

Mlle Skunk What? (*pause*) Did I call you Father?

M. Krap I rather thought so.

Mlle Skunk (*embarrassed*) Oh! (*Her lips tremble.*)

M. Krap Don't start again.

Mlle Skunk controls herself.

You can cry when you're alone.

Mlle Skunk Yes.

Silence.

M. Krap Hold on. I'm trying to get my ideas together. They're scattered. Like on a battlefield. (*pause*) Listen – I'm about to begin.

Mlle Skunk Don't go too fast.

M. Krap (*pedantically*) The mistake is to want to live. It isn't possible. There is nothing to live on in the life we have been lent. How absurd it is!

Mlle Skunk Yes.

M. Krap Isn't it? I resume. It's a question of materials. Either there are too many and we don't know where to start, or there are too few and there's no point in starting. But we do nevertheless start, because we're afraid of doing nothing. We sometimes even believe we are finishing, that does happen. And then we see it was only bluff. So we start again, with the too many and the too few. Why can't we be satisfied with a life that is only bluff? It must be because of its divine origin. People tell you that that's what life is, starting and re-starting. It isn't, though, it's merely the fear of doing nothing. Life isn't possible. I'm putting this badly.

Mlle Skunk I don't understand a word of it.

M. Krap That idiot of a doctor, with his abortions and his euthanasia. Did you hear him?

Mlle Skunk I wasn't really listening.

M. Krap A mechanic of the vilest sort.

Mlle Skunk I don't know what you mean when you talk about life and living. I don't understand Victor at all, either. Personally, I feel I'm living. Why do you want that to have a meaning?

M. Krap My God! She too thinks she can think!

Mlle Skunk Couldn't you quite simply say what you want?

M. Krap What I would have wanted?

Mlle Skunk If you prefer.

M. Krap I would have wanted to be contented, just for a moment.

Mlle Skunk But contented with what?

M. Krap With having been born, with not yet being dead.

Silence.

I'll conclude rapidly, because I can tell my wife's descending . . .

Mlle Skunk Your life is ending?

M. Krap My *wife*. That catastrophe. Is descending on us.

Mlle Skunk But . . .

M. Krap Just a moment. Being unable to live, then, but also being reluctant to resort to the ultimate remedy, either from decency or from cowardice, or precisely because he doesn't live, what can man do to avoid the madness – the modest, unobtrusive madness – that he has been taught to fear? (*pause*) He can pretend to live, and that other people live. (*Raises his hand.*) Just a moment. This is the solution, or rather the trick, that I have recently adopted. I'm not saying it's the only one. But I'm too old to learn from my . . . no, I won't name anyone. So there you have it. No, don't ask me any questions, I couldn't answer them. You smile, but I don't mind. You ought to smile more often. Except when you feel like it. That's what I do.

He opens his mouth wide in an enormous fixed grin.
Mlle Skunk shrinks back. End of grin.

Mlle Skunk You're horrible!

M. Krap Yes. One more thing.

Mlle Skunk No, no, I've had enough.

M. Krap I only want you to say yes.

Mlle Skunk Say yes? What to?

M. Krap To a little request.

Mlle Skunk No, no, I can't.

M. Krap Promise me. I'm dying.

  Silence.

Pretend to be alive for my son.

Mlle Skunk Yes, yes, anything you want.

M. Krap So that he can appear to be alive.

Mlle Skunk Yes, yes, I promise.

M. Krap You don't understand.

Mlle Skunk I promise, I promise.

  Silence.

M. Krap Won't you kiss me?

  Mlle Skunk starts crying again.

Never mind. You're right. But just don't cry. Wait
until . . .

  Enter Mme Krap.

M. Krap Wait until you're alone.

Mme Krap Are you ready, Olga?

Mlle Skunk In a moment. (*She stands up.*)

Mme Krap Where are you going?

Mlle Skunk To tidy up. (*Exit.*)

M. Krap She does understand.

Mme Krap Hurry up, Victor.

M. Krap Victor? My name is not Victor.

Mme Krap Hurry up. You haven't even shaved.

M. Krap I'm not going out.

Mme Krap (*taking him by the arm*) Come on, get a move on, stand up.

M. Krap Don't make me have to kill you, Violette.

Mme Krap Kill me! You! Kill me! Me! (*Laughs heartily.*)

M. Krap (*taking a razor out of his pocket*) Help me up.

　Mme Krap retreats.

I would have preferred (*he tries to rise*) to leave you to your cancer. But never mind. (*He half rises.*)

Mme Krap (*retreating towards the door*) You're completely mad!

M. Krap (*still stuck in his chair*) Once I'm up, there'll be no problem.

Mme Krap (*realising that he can't get up*) You impotent old fool! (*Moving back to him.*) And to think that you frightened me for a moment!

M. Krap (*letting himself fall back*) Not easy to sit up, even to kill your wife.

Mme Krap Monster!

M. Krap Me too?

Mme Krap Bastard!

M. Krap And, anyway, just you wait and see. I'll cut your throat tonight, while you're snoring.

Mme Krap (*terrified at the horizons opening up before her, and perhaps especially at the idea of spending an uneasy evening with her guests*) Don't be like that, Henri! Think of all we've been through together! Of our great sorrow! Let's be friends!

M. Krap (*affably*) Sit down for a second.

Mme Krap sits down.

Did you see Victor?

Mme Krap I swear I didn't. I simply went for a walk. I was on edge. I've already told you so.

M. Krap What did he say?

Enter Mlle Skunk.

Mme Krap Wait for me a moment, Olga. I'll be with you in a second.

Exit Mlle Skunk.

M. Krap You don't have to admit you're lying, or even make excuses. Simply tell me what he said.

Mme Krap (*with an effort*) He said he never wanted to see me again.

M. Krap How were you with him?

Mme Krap How was I? I don't understand.

M. Krap You acted the worried mother.

Mme Krap I am terribly worried.

M. Krap And then threatening. And then grief-stricken.

Silence.

For the five-hundredth time.

Silence.

You begged, you shouted, you wept.

Silence. Violently:

Answer me!

Mme Krap Of course, Henri, as you know very well.

M. Krap (*reassured*) That's perfect.

Mme Krap stands up.

Just a moment.

Mme Krap sits down again.

And you threatened to cut off his allowance?

Mme Krap Yes, I told him that things couldn't go on like this.

M. Krap That's a new one.

Mme Krap I had already hinted at it.

M. Krap But without driving him into a corner?

Mme Krap Yes.

M. Krap Was it today that you were supposed to take him the money?

Mme Krap Yes.

M. Krap Then why did you invite Jeanne?

Mme Krap I wanted her to come with me.

M. Krap And then Marguerite came?

56

Mme Krap Yes.

M. Krap Did you see Jeanne before she left?

Mme Krap Yes.

M. Krap But you didn't say anything to her?

Mme Krap No. She was furious.

M. Krap Did you give it to him?

Mme Krap What's that?

M. Krap Did you give him the money?

Mme Krap No.

M. Krap What did he say?

Mme Krap That it didn't matter.

M. Krap And that he never wanted to see you again?

Mme Krap Yes.

M. Krap That's good, very good.

> *He rubs his hands. Mme Krap cries. Handkerchief. She controls herself.*

Oh, have you already stopped?

Mme Krap One shouldn't let oneself go.

M. Krap On the contrary, one should, one should, it's . . . (*He interrupts himself, struck by a painful thought.*) But what are you going to do now?

Mme Krap What am I going to do?

M. Krap You won't go and see him any more?

Mme Krap I don't know.

M. Krap But you have no more trump cards. (*pause*)
Unless you think up something else.

Mme Krap We shall think up something else all right.
Things can't go on like this.

M. Krap Bravo!

Mme Krap Can they?

M. Krap But of course we'll think up something else.

Mme Krap stands up.

To let them go on like this.

Mme Krap What now?

M. Krap Just one more little question and I'll have
finished.

Mme Krap (*sitting down again*) I'm late.

M. Krap They can wait.

Silence.

How many times did you try to get rid of him?

Mme Krap (*in a low voice*) Three times.

M. Krap But it didn't work?

Mme Krap It just made me feel queasy.

M. Krap Just queasy! (*pause*) And then you said . . . what
was it . . . what was the charming way you put it?

Mme Krap The charming way I put it?

M. Krap Yes . . . what was it . . . 'Since he's there . . .'

Mme Krap 'Let's keep him, since he's there.'

M. Krap (*vivaciously*) That's it! That's it! 'Let's keep him
since he's there.' (*pause*) We were on the water. Your

boater had an osprey in it. I had stopped rowing. We were being gently rocked by the waves. (*pause*) He too was being gently rocked by the waves. (*pause*) Are you sure he's mine?

Mme Krap (*after some thought*) There are . . . um . . . seventy chances out of a hundred.

M. Krap My stock is rising.

Mme Krap Is that all?

M. Krap Oh yes, that's all.

Mme Krap (*rising*) And you aren't still angry with me, Henri?

M. Krap Angry? On the contrary. I am very pleased with you, Violette, very pleased. You have been splendid, absolutely natural.

Mme Krap Have a good evening. (*She starts to go out.*)

M. Krap Violette!

Mme Krap (*stopping*) Yes?

M. Krap Won't you kiss me?

Mme Krap Oh, not now, Henri, I'm so late.

M. Krap That's true.

Mme Krap (*mischievously*) And then, you know, I am still a little bit afraid of your razor! (*Exit.*)

Fairly long silence.

M. Krap To keep the punters amused!

Silence. A knock. Silence. Another knock. Silence. Enter Jacques.

Jacques Monsieur is served.

M. Krap Now what do you want?

Jacques Monsieur is served.

M. Krap Monsieur has been served right.

Jacques Would monsieur prefer me to serve him here?

M. Krap Serve him what?

Jacques But monsieur's dinner.

M. Krap Ah yes, dinner. (*Reflects.*) I won't have any dinner.

Jacques (*distressed*) Will monsieur not have anything?

M. Krap Not this evening.

Jacques Does monsieur not feel well?

M. Krap No worse than usual.

  Silence.

Jacques Would monsieur not like to listen to a little music?

M. Krap Music?

Jacques It often does monsieur good.

  Silence.

The Kopek Quartet is playing at the moment, monsieur. We are listening to it in the servants' quarters. It is a very fine programme, monsieur.

M. Krap What?

Jacques Schubert, monsieur.

  Silence.

I could relay it to the large salon, monsieur, and leave the doors open, monsieur does not like it to be too loud.

60

M. Krap Please yourself.

Exit Jacques. Music. It's the Andante from the A flat Quartet. For a good minute, if possible. M. Krap becomes increasingly agitated. Then, with all his strength:

Jacques! Jacques!

He tries to stand up. Music. Jacques comes running in.

Stop it! Stop it!

Exit Jacques. Music. The music stops.

What an abomination!

Enter Jacques.

Jacques Does monsieur not like it?

M. Krap's agitation gradually decreases.

I am so sorry, monsieur.

Silence.

Is there anything monsieur would like?

M. Krap Don't leave me.

Jacques Of course not, monsieur.

M. Krap Talk to me a little.

Jacques Is there anything that particularly interests monsieur?

Silence.

Has monsieur seen the papers?

M. Krap I saw them yesterday.

Jacques What does monsieur think of the new government?

M. Krap No, no, not that.

Silence.

Jacques Has monsieur any encouraging news of monsieur's son?

Silence.

M. Krap When is the marriage to be?

Jacques Monsieur means, Marie and me?

M. Krap Yes.

Jacques In a month or two, we hope, monsieur.

M. Krap Do you already make love?

Jacques We . . . er . . . I . . . er . . . not exactly love, monsieur.

M. Krap I haven't offended you?

Jacques Oh, monsieur!

M. Krap You're rather obsequious, Jacques.

Jacques I quite enjoy grovelling, monsieur.

M. Krap Then you're right.

Marie appears at the door.

Marie Madame is asking for monsieur on the telephone.

M. Krap Come a bit closer, Marie.

Marie advances.

Closer still.

Marie goes and stands by the floor lamp.

Turn round.

Marie turns round.

62

She's sweet.

Marie What am I to tell madame, monsieur?

M. Krap That I'm coming.

Marie Very good, monsieur. (*Exit.*)

M. Krap I don't suppose you get bored.

Jacques From time to time, monsieur.

M. Krap Take the call.

Jacques Very good, monsieur.

Exit. M. Krap motionless. Enter Jacques.

Madame was asking after monsieur, and wishes him to know that Doctor Piouk is extremely sorry that monsieur did not accompany madame. Doctor Piouk had a great many things to say to monsieur.

M. Krap Did you hang up?

Jacques Yes, monsieur, I thought it best.

Silence.

M. Krap Jacques.

Jacques Yes, monsieur.

M. Krap I would like you to kiss me.

Jacques Certainly, monsieur. On monsieur's cheeks?

M. Krap Wherever you like.

Jacques kisses M. Krap.

Jacques Again, monsieur?

M. Krap No, thank you.

Jacques Very good, monsieur. (*He straightens up.*)

63

M. Krap Here. (*Gives him a hundred-franc note.*)

Jacques (*taking it*) Oh, you shouldn't have, monsieur.

M. Krap You're prickly.

Jacques Monsieur also is a little prickly.

M. Krap You kiss nicely.

Jacques I do my best, monsieur.

   Silence.

M. Krap I ought to have been a homosexual.

   Silence.

What do you think of it?

Jacques Of what, monsieur?

M. Krap Of homosexuality.

Jacques I think it must come to more or less the same thing, monsieur.

M. Krap You are a cynic.

   Silence.

Jacques Am I to stay with monsieur?

M. Krap No, you can abandon me.

Jacques Would monsieur not do better to go to bed?

   Silence.

Is there nothing else I can do for monsieur?

M. Krap No. Yes. Put out that abominable light.

Jacques Very good, monsieur. (*He switches the floor lamp off.*) I will leave the little lamp on, monsieur.

   Silence.

Good night, monsieur.

M. Krap Good night.

Jacques starts to go out.

Leave the doors open.

Jacques Very good, monsieur.

M. Krap So that you can hear my cries.

Jacques Very good, mons . . . I beg your pardon, monsieur?

M. Krap Leave them open.

Jacques Very good, monsieur. (*Exit, worried.*)

M. Krap motionless.

M. Krap Curtain.

M. Krap motionless.

CURTAIN

Act II

Next day. Late afternoon.

    Victor's room, a squalid bed-sitting-room whose only piece of furniture is a folding bed.

    Victor, alone. Sordidly dressed, in his socks, he is walking up and down. He stops near the footlights, looks at the audience, is about to speak, changes his mind, starts walking again. He halts again at the footlights, trying to find the right words, ill at ease.

Victor I must tell . . . I'm not . . .

    He falls silent, starts walking again, picks up a shoe and throws it through the window pane. Enter, immediately, a glazier, with his tool kit and with Victor's shoe in his hand. He throws the shoe down and starts work.

Impossible to break anything.

Glazier But you have broken it.

Victor You can't lose anything, either.

    Enter a young boy, carrying a tin.

Glazier This is my assistant. He carries the putty. Don't you, Michel?

Michel Yes, Papa.

Glazier Yes, monsieur.

Michel Yes, monsieur.

Glazier Have you got the diamond?

Michel No, monsieur.

Glazier Tsk-tsk! Go and get the diamond, quick.

Michel Yes, monsieur. (*He starts to go out.*)

Glazier Don't take the putty with you.

Michel puts the tin down on the floor by the window and goes out.

He was taking the putty with him! (*Scrapes.*) Little scatterbrain! And the diamond. (*Scrapes.*) What am I supposed to do without a diamond? (*Turning round to Victor:*) Without a diamond I am nothing, monsieur.

Enter Michel.

You took your time. Have you got it?

Michel Yes, monsieur.

Glazier Come over here. Right by me. Ready?

Michel Yes, monsieur.

Glazier I don't talk like a glazier, do I?

Victor I don't know.

Glazier You can take my word for it.

Victor Did they send you to spy on me?

Glazier Had you not broken the window, I would not be here.

Silence. The glazier works.

You see, monsieur, what is admirable about me is that I'm useless.

Victor You're useful for repairing my window.

Glazier True, but you will break it again tomorrow. At least, I hope so.

Victor It's pointless for me to break the window, and it's pointless for you to repair it.

Glazier True again!

Victor The simplest thing would be not to start.

Glazier (*turning round*) Ah, monsieur, don't talk nonsense!

Enter Mme Karl, an old woman.

Mme Karl You've broken the window.

Glazier His shoe went straight through it, madame.

Mme Karl It's the general's lady.

Victor The general's lady?

Mme Karl Yes.

Victor Tell her I'm out.

Mme Karl I did. She won't go.

Victor Then she'll have to stay.

Mme Karl She's on her way up.

Victor You must stop her!

Mme Karl There's two men with her. Her chauffeur and another one.

Victor I'll go down.

Mme Karl It's too late. (*She goes out on to the landing. Comes back.*) She's on the third floor. She's panting.

Victor Is she alone?

Mme Karl I told you, there's two men with her.

Glazier Her chauffeur and another man, unidentified.

Victor What am I to do?

Glazier Hide.

Victor Where?

Glazier Under the bed.

Victor You think so?

Glazier Quick! Quick! Under the bed!

Victor hides under the bed.

Mme Karl Here she is.

Enter Mme Meck. She looks round for Victor.

I told you he wasn't here.

Glazier Allow me, madame, to make myself known. I am the so-called glazier. And this is young Michel, my so-called assistant. He carries the putty. Say how do you do to the lady, Michel.

Exit Mme Karl.

Michel How do you do, madame?

Mme Meck Have you seen monsieur Krap?

Glazier Monsieur Krap?

Mme Meck The young man who lives here.

Glazier Ah, the young man who lives here.

Mme Meck Have you seen him?

Glazier Yes, madame.

Mme Meck Where is he?

Glazier He is under the bed, madame, as in Molière's day.

Victor emerges from under the bed.

69

You should have stayed there.

Mme Meck What is all this buffoonery?

Glazier Its purpose is to provide public relaxation and entertainment, madame.

Victor What do you want with me?

Mme Meck What a dear little boy. Come and say how do you do to me, my little fellow. He looks like a real little man.

Glazier May I ask you to leave my assistant in peace, madame? He has already said how do you do to you. Can't you see he is holding the putty?

Mme Meck You are not very amiable.

Glazier There is a time for work, madame, and there is a time for amiabilities. Michel must learn at an early stage to distinguish the one from the other.

Mme Meck Is he your son?

Glazier When I am working, I have no family, madame.

Mme Meck You call this working? You do nothing but talk.

Glazier My brain never ceases to work.

Mme Meck (*to Victor*) He is rather like your poor papa, when he was younger.

Glazier Really?

Mme Meck Stop meddling in our affairs.

Glazier But you have been meddling in mine.

Mme Meck (*to Victor*) Aren't you going to offer me a chair?

Victor There aren't any chairs.

Mme Meck There was one, last time.

Victor There isn't, now.

Mme Meck sits down on the bed.

What do you want?

Mme Meck The resemblance is truly striking.

Victor Have you brought me some money?

Mme Meck I have come to see you.

Victor I'm going out.

Mme Meck I'll come with you.

She stands up. Victor goes over to the door, opens it, stands there for a moment, disconcerted, goes out on to the landing.

Victor's voice Madame Karl!

Silence.

Madame Karl!

Victor comes back and shuts the door.

Mme Meck You aren't going out, then?

Victor Not just yet.

Mme Meck sits down again.

Who is that man on the landing?

Mme Meck That's Joseph.

Victor Is he with you?

Mme Meck He's a fifth-rate wrestler. Ludovic used to employ him from time to time.

71

Victor Is he with you?

Mme Meck Yes, Victor, he is with me.

The glazier goes over to the door, opens it, looks outside.

Glazier Come and look, Michel.

Michel goes over to the door. Both look out of it for quite a while. The glazier shuts the door quietly and goes back to work. Michel follows him.

He must take size 48 in shoes.

Michel What's that on his nose, Papa?

Glazier Monsieur.

Michel Monsieur.

Glazier I don't know, Michel, what that is on his nose. There are so many things you can have on your nose. Ask him, if you want to know. Or rather, ask this good lady, that would be wiser.

Michel What's that on his nose, madame?

Mme Meck It is the result of a bite, my child.

Michel Was it a dog that bit him, madame?

Mme Meck No, my child, it was a man, a fellow creature.

Michel Why did he bite him, madame?

Mme Meck To make him let go, my child.

Glazier That's enough! That's enough! This is getting us nowhere. Pass me the rule.

Michel But you've already got it, monsieur.

Glazier So I have. (*He starts measuring.*)

Victor Why is that man with you?

72

Mme Meck To remove you by force, if need be.

Victor By force?

Mme Meck You are not very amenable to reason, I think.

Enter Mme Karl.

Mme Karl What do you want?

Victor I want my bill. I'm leaving you.

Mme Karl What did you say?

Victor I said I'm leaving you and I want my bill.

Mme Karl You have to give a week's notice.

Victor Just make out a bill for whatever you think I owe you. I'm leaving today.

Mme Karl What have you got to complain about?

Victor I'm quite willing to tell you, madame Karl. I'm complaining about being constantly disturbed. Yesterday it was my mother, today it's the general's widow, tomorrow it will be my fiancée. I can't even break my window without a glazier suddenly materialising and starting to repair it – and so terribly slowly.

Mme Karl You shouldn't have given them your address.

Victor I didn't give it to them. They found it.

Mme Karl But wherever you go they'll still find you.

Victor That's not so sure.

Mme Karl (*to Mme Meck*) Can't you leave him in peace?

Mme Meck Mind your own business.

Victor Madame Karl, do me a favour, bring me the bill. It's no use arguing with these people.

73

Mme Karl It's a disgrace. (*She starts to go out.*)

Victor Oh, Madame Karl!

Mme Karl What?

Victor Is Thérèse downstairs?

Mme Karl Yes.

Victor Ask her to go and fetch a policeman and bring him here.

Mme Karl A policeman? Whatever for? I don't want any cops in my house.

Victor This lady is trespassing on my domicile.

Mme Karl You're big enough to throw her out.

Victor She's brought a bodyguard with her. He's on the landing, and only waiting for the signal to intervene.

Mme Meck Joseph!

Enter Joseph.

Do what you have to do.

Joseph Is that him?

Mme Meck Yes.

Joseph (*taking Victor by the arm*) Come on.

Victor Help!

Mme Karl Help!

Joseph Shut your trap. (*He gives her a push.*)

Victor Let me go!

He struggles feebly. Joseph drags him over to the door.

Glazier (*to Michel*) Pass me the hammer.

Michel But you've already got it, monsieur.

Glazier So I have.

He goes up to Joseph and hits him on the head with the hammer. Joseph falls down.

Mme Meck This is ridiculous.

The glazier goes back to his work.

Mme Karl (*on her way out*) I'm going for a policeman.

Mme Meck He's killed him.

Victor There's no need now, Madame Karl.

Mme Karl Charges must be brought.

Victor Tell the chauffeur to come up.

Mme Karl He hit me.

Victor The chauffeur, Madame Karl, the chauffeur. You'll get compensation.

Mme Karl What a way to go on. (*Exit.*)

Mme Meck Violence proved useless.

Victor You make my life impossible. You cover me with shame and ridicule. Go away.

Mme Meck Your life? What life? You are dead.

Victor No one hounds the dead.

Mme Meck You know your aunt is in Paris?

Victor My mother told me.

Mme Meck She is married to a . . .

Victor My mother told me.

Mme Meck You know you have broken your mother's heart?

Victor Yes, she told me. Go away.

Mme Meck But you don't care?

Victor I can't help it.

Mme Meck You could go home.

Victor I can't go home.

Mme Meck You could live differently.

Victor I can't live differently.

Mme Meck You know Olga is sick with grief?

Victor Yes, she told me and my mother confirmed it.

Mme Meck Have you no more feeling for her?

Victor No.

Mme Meck Nor for anyone?

Victor No.

Mme Meck Except for yourself.

Victor Not even for myself.

Glazier The picture is beginning to emerge.

Mme Meck What are you going to pay your bill with?

Victor With the money I have left.

Mme Meck And after that?

Victor I shall manage.

Mme Meck Your father is dead.

Silence.

76

Glazier Say something for goodness' sake!

A knock. Enter Thomas.

Mme Meck See to your colleague.

He goes over to Joseph.

Thomas Madame?

Mme Meck See if he is breathing. You are used to mechanics.

Thomas (*after examining Joseph*) Yes, madame.

Mme Meck Is he breathing?

Thomas Yes, madame.

Mme Meck Drag him out on to the landing.

Thomas Very good, madame. (*He drags Joseph out on to the landing, comes back.*)

Mme Meck Try and bring him round.

Thomas Very good, madame.

Mme Meck As soon as he can walk, both of you go down and wait for me in the car.

Chauffeur Very good, madame. (*Exit.*)

Silence.

Mme Meck Victor!

Silence.

Did you hear me? Your father is dead.

Victor (*turning round*) Yes. When did he die?

Mme Meck You are not going to tell me that you're interested?

Victor The time interests me.

Mme Meck He died yesterday evening, in his armchair.

Victor But at what time?

Mme Meck He was alive at eight o'clock. Jacques is sure of that. And he was found dead at about midnight.

Victor Who found him?

Mme Meck Your poor mother.

Victor At midnight?

Mme Meck About then.

Victor Was he stiff?

Mme Meck You are completely unnatural.

Silence.

Your mother is prostrate.

Glazier (*to Michel*) The diamond. (*to Victor:*) Haven't you got a table?

Victor No.

Glazier Ah, well. (*He starts to cut his glass on the floor.*)

Victor (*to Mme Meck*) Go away.

A knock. Enter Thomas.

Thomas I can't bring him round, madame.

Mme Meck Is he still breathing?

Thomas Yes, madame, but I can't bring him round.

Mme Meck He is probably too heavy for you to carry.

Thomas I'm afraid he is, madame.

Mme Meck (*to Victor*) I don't suppose you would like to help Thomas carry Joseph down to the car, would you?

Victor No.

Mme Meck (*to the glazier*) What about you?

   Silence.

Glazier!

Glazier (*without turning round, going on working*) Madame?

Mme Meck I don't suppose you would like to help Thomas carry Joseph down to the car, would you?

Glazier No, madame, I would not like to.

Mme Meck Well, Thomas, you will have to send for an ambulance.

Thomas Very good, madame. (*Exit.*)

Victor (*to Mme Meck*) Go away.

Mme Meck But you can put me out, now.

Victor I couldn't bear to touch you.

Mme Meck (*going down on her knees*) Victor! Come back home! With me! In the Delage!

Victor Get up.

Mme Meck Help me.

   Victor helps her up with the tips of his fingers.

The will . . .

Glazier Shit! I've cut it too short.

Victor (*to the glazier*) Forget it, then.

Glazier (*nobly*) I shall repair this window if it takes me the rest of my life.

Mme Meck It is going to be read tomorrow, after the funeral.

Glazier Pass me the rule.

Michel But you've already got it.

Glazier Monsieur.

Michel Monsieur.

Glazier So I have.

Mme Meck Your mother is prostrate.

Silence.

She is asking for you.

Silence.

Her sole support!

The glazier laughs hilariously. Which makes him drop his rule.

Glazier Pass me the rule.

Michel passes it to him.

Victor (*to Mme Meck*) Go away.

He picks up her handbag and holds it out to her, then her umbrella, which he uses to prod her towards the door.

Mme Meck Wretch!

Victor (*still prodding*) Go on.

Mme Meck Give me my umbrella.

Victor Go on, get out!

He pushes her out, gives her her umbrella, shuts the door, comes back and sits on the bed.

Silence.

Glazier She'll be back.

Victor (*half turning towards the audience, with a gesture of helplessness*) I . . .

Glazier Peace at last.

Victor Are you going to be much longer?

Glazier The thing is, I can't see properly.

Victor Go away.

Glazier I'll put the light on. (*He goes over to the switch and flips it. Nothing happens.*) There's no bulb. Quick, Michel, go and fetch a bulb.

Michel Yes, monsieur. (*Exit.*)

Glazier (*going over to the bed*) You don't like things made of glass.

Victor Go away.

Glazier Oh, me, you know, once I get stuck into anything, there's no stopping me. Can't be helped, that's the way I am.

Victor If I had the guts, I'd try to throw you out.

Glazier But you're afraid?

Victor Yes.

Glazier What of?

Victor Of getting hurt.

Silence.

Glazier You know, it's time you explained yourself.

Victor Explained myself?

Glazier Of course. Things can't go on like this.

Victor But it's all beyond me. What's more I don't owe you any explanations. Who are you? I don't know you. Chuck it in. (*pause*) And fuck off.

Glazier But you should, you should, it would do you good to explain yourself.

Victor (*yelling*) I tell you it's all beyond me.

Glazier Explain yourself, no, that's not what I mean, I put it badly. Define yourself, that's it. It's time you defined yourself. You sit there like a kind of . . . how can I put it? Like a kind of oozing pus. Like a kind of sanies, that's it. Get a bit of body, for God's sake.

Victor Why?

Glazier So that the whole thing can look as if it makes some sort of sense. So far you've been impossible. No one could believe it . . . But you're quite simply nothing, my poor friend.

Victor Maybe it's time that something was quite simply nothing.

Glazier Oh, yes, I know, I've heard it all before. All this is nothing but words. Listen. When she . . .

Enter Michel.

When she told you . . . What do *you* want?

Michel The bulb, monsieur.

Glazier Well, put it in! When she told you . . .

Michel Where do I put it, monsieur?

Glazier Where do you put it! Why in the . . . in the . . . in the whatsit, of course, not in your behind, in the . . . in the *socket*, that's the word, put it in the socket, and not in your

82

pocket, either, and don't knock it, idiot. (*pause*) Basically, it's only words that interest me. I'm a poet who prefers not to know it. (*to Michel*) Well, have you done it?

Michel I can't do it, monsieur.

Glazier You can call me Papa for the moment, this is our break.

Michel It's too high, Papa.

Glazier Stand on a chair.

Michel There aren't any chairs, Papa.

Glazier Nor there are. Stand on the tool box, then.

Michel drags the tool box over to the socket, stands on it, inserts the bulb, gets down.

Now switch on.

Michel goes over to the door, flips the switch, the bulb lights up.

It works.

Victor (*half standing up*) I'm going.

Glazier Switch off.

Michel switches the light off. Victor falls back on to the bed.

Come here. Bring the tool box. (*He sits down on the box in front of Victor, puts his arm round Michel and cuddles him.*)

Michel What's the matter with him, Papa?

Glazier Who says there's anything the matter with him?

Michel He looks funny.

Glazier He *is* funny.

Michel Is it because his papa is dead?

Glazier How do you know his papa is dead?

Michel The fat lady said so.

Glazier She may have been lying. (*pause*) Take a good look at him, Michel.

Michel Why would the lady have lied, Papa?

Glazier To get him to go home with her, for goodness' sake. And then, once they'd got him there, they would have locked him up. (*pause*) Take a good look at him (*pause*) You won't be like that when you're grown up, will you, Michel?

Michel Oh no, Papa.

Enter Mme Karl.

Mme Karl (*to the glazier*) Haven't you finished yet?

Glazier No, madame, I haven't finished yet, and I'm not likely to finish yet, either, at this rate.

Mme Karl (*to Victor*) Here's the bill. (*Advances to the bed.*) Here.

Victor takes the bill without enthusiasm and keeps it in his hand without looking at it.

Well, then, are you leaving, yes or no?

Silence.

Are you ill?

Glazier Give him time to think.

Victor (*with an effort*) Madame Karl, I'd like nothing better than to stay here, but I must be left in peace.

Glazier People come in here as and when they please. It's unbelievable. They don't even knock.

Mme Karl What am I supposed to do when they come with their hatchet men? They all know he's here. He shouldn't have given them his address.

Glazier Incidentally, is Tarzan still on the landing?

Mme Karl No, he's gone.

Glazier In the ambulance?

Mme Karl No, he went on his own. On foot.

Glazier (*rubbing his hands*) Peace at last.

Victor You wouldn't have another room?

Mme Karl What difference would that make?

Victor You could say I'm not here any more, and I'd be in the other room.

Mme Karl All the rooms are occupied.

Glazier And why don't you lock yourself in?

Victor There's no lock.

Glazier No lock! (*to Mme Karl:*) Aren't you ashamed of yourself, letting rooms without locks?

Mme Karl He didn't have to take it. No one forced him.

Glazier But can't you see what a . . . what a wreck you're dealing with? (*to Michel:*) Quick, go and fetch a lock.

Michel Yes, Papa.

Glazier Monsieur.

Michel Yes, monsieur. (*Exit.*)

Glazier We'll sort that out for you.

85

Victor They'll break the door down.

Mme Karl Well? Are you leaving, yes or no?

Glazier But give him time to breathe, for goodness' sake.

Victor I'll tell you later.

Mme Karl I'll give you an hour. Then I'll put up the notice. (*Exit.*)

  Silence.

Glazier Hadn't you thought about that?

Victor Leave me alone. Don't say any more. Do what you have to do and get out.

Glazier Yes, but tell me first: hadn't you thought about that?

Victor Of course I had.

Glazier About having a lock fitted?

Victor Of course I had.

Glazier That's not what I'm talking about! What I mean is, hadn't you thought that the old woman might have been lying when she told you your father was dead?

Victor She wasn't lying.

  Silence. Enter Michel.

Glazier Where have you been dawdling again?

Michel I wasn't dawdling, Papa.

Glazier Have you got the lock?

Michel Yes, monsieur.

Glazier And two keys?

Michel Yes, monsieur.

Glazier Good. (*He stands up. To Victor:*) As for you, I have no more to say to you. I've come across plenty of ham actors but never one as bad as you. If you were absolutely determined to get yourself booed you couldn't have done any better. You get the words put into your mouth and you come out with the complete opposite. Have you no more feeling for your mother? No. Nor for your fiancée? No. Nor for anyone? No. Only for yourself? Not even for yourself. But what is all this bullshit? We need feelings, for Christ's sake! Naturally you love your mother, naturally you love your fiancée, but . . . *but* you have your duties – to yourself, to your work, to science, to the party, to I don't know what else, which make you a man apart, an exceptional being, which don't allow you to enjoy the pleasures of family relationships, of passion, which clap a cellophane mask over your face. To have feelings, to have feelings – and then to reject them, that's your mission! To sacrifice everything, to your fixed idea, to your vocation! And only then do you start living. No one would want to lynch you any more. You are the model of the poor young man, the heroic young man. People see you dying like a dog at thirty, thirty-three, exhausted by your labours, by your discoveries, ravaged by radium, prostrated by sleepless nights and privation, killed in the performance of your duty, shot by Franco, shot by Stalin. Everyone applauds you. Your mother dies of a broken heart, so does your fiancée, but what does that matter, we need men like you, men of ideals, above comfort, above pity, so that people will go on buying ice-creams. (*Imitating him:*) No . . . no . . . she told me . . . I don't want anything . . . I can't do anything . . . I don't feel anything . . . I am nothing . . . leave me alone . . . go away . . . please . . . *please.* Shit! (*to Michel:*) Switch the light on. But what good are you doing?

Victor What?

Michel switches the light on.

Glazier I asked you what good you're doing by rotting in this lousy dump?

Victor I don't know.

Glazier I don't know, I don't know! Oh, run away and hide.

Victor I wish I could.

Glazier (*to Michel*) Give me the rule.

Michel But you've already got it, monsieur.

Glazier (*thundering*) No, I have not got it! (*to Victor:*) Where do you find the nerve and the strength to push old ladies out with umbrellas?

Victor I defend my property, when I can.

Glazier Your property! What property?

Victor My liberty.

Glazier Your liberty! That's a good one, your liberty! Liberty to do what?

Victor To do nothing.

Glazier (*controlling himself with an effort, to Michel*) The rule.

Michel Here, monsieur.

Glazier What shall we do? Do we finish the window or fix the lock or forget the whole thing?

Michel I'm hungry, Papa.

Glazier You're hungry, Papa. Let's do the lock first, then.

He goes to work. Silence. He sings:

Our France is fair,
Her fate is blest,

   (*to Michel:*) Sing!

Glazier and **Michel** (*in chorus*)
Our France is fair,
Her fate is blest,
We'll unite for her
And live our best.
O'er hill and dale, o'er . . .

   Enter Mlle Skunk. She goes and stands in front of Victor,
   who is still sitting on his bed.

Mlle Skunk Hallo, Victor.

Victor Hallo.

Mlle Skunk Who is that man?

Victor He's a glazier.

Mlle Skunk What is he doing here?

Victor He's repairing the window.

Mlle Skunk Did you break the window?

Victor What?

Mlle Skunk Was it you who broke the window?

Victor Yes.

Mlle Skunk How? Why?

Victor I don't know.

Glazier With his shoe, mademoiselle, deliberately. There's still hope.

Mlle Skunk Why did you do it?

Victor What?

Mlle Skunk Why did you break the window?

Victor I don't know.

Glazier Come with me, Michel.

Exeunt the glazier and Michel.

Mlle Skunk Aren't you going to kiss me?

Victor No.

Mlle Skunk Aren't I attractive?

Victor I don't know.

Mlle Skunk You used to find me attractive, in the old days. You wanted to sleep with me.

Victor In the old days.

Mlle Skunk Don't you want to sleep with me any more?

Victor No.

Mlle Skunk Who with, then?

Victor What?

Mlle Skunk Who do you want to sleep with now?

Victor No one.

Mlle Skunk But that's not possible!

Silence.

You aren't telling the truth!

Silence.

You know that I love you?

Victor So you've told me.

Mlle Skunk Don't you feel sorry for me?

Victor No.

Mlle Skunk Do you want me to leave?

Victor Yes.

Mlle Skunk And never come back?

Victor Yes.

   Silence.

Mlle Skunk What has changed you so much?

Victor I don't know.

Mlle Skunk You used not to be like this. What has made you like this?

Victor I don't know. (*pause*) I've always been like this.

Mlle Skunk You haven't! It's not true! You used to love me. You used to work. You used to have a joke with your father. You used to travel. You . . .

Victor It was bluff. But that's enough! Go away.

   Enter the glazier and Michel.

Glazier I was trying to be discreet, tactful, a man of the world, but I see there's no way. So I'll get on with my work. For every moment is precious. If you don't mind. (*to Michel:*) Pass me the . . . (*He finds it.*) Hold the door. (*He goes to work.*)

Mlle Skunk Your father is dead.

Victor So Jeanne told me.

Mlle Skunk Jeanne was here?

Victor Yes.

Mlle Skunk When?

Victor Just now.

Silence.

Mlle Skunk Doesn't it affect you?

Victor What?

Mlle Skunk That your father is dead?

Silence.

Do you know what he said to me yesterday evening?

Silence.

He made me promise to pretend to be alive so that you too could appear to be alive. I don't understand.

Silence.

That is why I came, to ask you to tell me what it means.

Silence.

Do you understand what it means?

Victor No.

Mlle Skunk You aren't even trying to.

Victor No.

Mlle Skunk Why not?

Victor Everything can be understood.

Mlle Skunk Tell me, then.

Victor (*furiously*) No!

Silence.

Mlle Skunk He asked me to kiss him. (*pause*) I couldn't.

Victor But you want me to kiss you.

Glazier (*turning round*) Well well. There may be something to be done along those lines. It isn't the line I would have chosen myself, it will never get us very far, but even so it may be better than nothing. (*to Mlle Skunk:*) Don't you see, mademoiselle – what he cannot or will not understand is that he isn't convincing. I shall never weary of repeating that. (*pause*) But if it was for love of his father that he . . . (*He interrupts himself.*) No, that wouldn't lead anywhere. Unless . . . (*pause*) Well, no harm in giving it a go. (*to Mlle Skunk:*) Try and get at him along those lines. The poor old boy, jeered at by his wife, abandoned by his son, ridiculous in his work, grievously ill, who feels his end is near, he asks you to kiss him and you don't want to. Then what?

Mlle Skunk I don't understand a word you're saying. You talk like him.

Glazier Like whom?

Mlle Skunk Like his father.

Glazier But of course! Well. That's your problem. To work. Every moment is precious. (*to Michel:*) Hold the door steady. Wedge it with your foot. That's it. (*He starts work again.*)

Mlle Skunk (*to Victor*) Do you understand what he's trying to say?

Victor No.

Silence.

Go away. I'm tired.

Mlle Skunk (*standing up*) I'm going.

Silence.

Will you be staying here?

Victor I'm going to try to sleep.

Mlle Skunk No, I mean: in future, are you going to stay here?

Victor No, I shall go somewhere else.

Mlle Skunk Where?

Victor I don't know.

Silence.

Mlle Skunk Marguerite is back.

Silence.

She's married.

Silence.

To a doctor.

Victor lies down.

He flirts with me.

Silence.

Do you know what he said to me?

Silence. Mlle Skunk stamps her foot.

Answer me, for once!

Victor I don't understand.

Mlle Skunk What? What don't you understand?

Victor What you want to know.

Mlle Skunk But I don't want to know anything. I simply want you to listen to me.

Victor I'm listening. I thought you were leaving.

Mlle Skunk I told him I wished I was dead. He told me

that that would be easy and that he'd be glad to help me.

Glazier Funny way to flirt.

Victor Who?

Mlle Skunk The doctor.

Victor What doctor?

Mlle Skunk Marguerite's husband, of course. I've just told you.

Victor I didn't know she was married.

Silence.

Glazier Watch out! Someone's coming up. (*He goes out on to the landing, comes back.*) It's a real lady. I saw her hat. I smelt her perfume. She's coming upstairs, taking care not to touch the banisters. She's not alone.

He shuts the door and leans against it. Silence. A knock. Silence. Another knock. Silence. The door is pushed. The glazier braces his back against it, resisting the pressure. He signs to Michel to help him. Michel helps him.

She's as strong as an ox. (*pause*) They're conferring. (*pause*) To open or not to open, that is the . . . (*to Michel:*) Well?

Michel That is the question.

Glazier They're trying again. (*to Michel:*) Push. (*They push. To Mlle Skunk:*) Help us.

Voice Open the door!

Mlle Skunk It's him!

Glazier Who?

Mlle Skunk The doctor!

95

The glazier abruptly moves away from the door, which bursts open and sends Michel flying. Dr Piouk comes rushing into the room and falls over on to his knees. Same business with Mme Piouk, who is following him. Mme Meck is in the doorway. Dr Piouk gets up.

Dr Piouk (*to the glazier*) Are you responsible for this schoolboy prank?

Glazier We have to keep the punters amused.

Mme Piouk Help me up.

Mlle Skunk helps her up.

Dr Piouk You haven't hurt yourself, darling?

Glazier (*to Michel*) You haven't hurt yourself, dearest?

Michel No, Papa.

Glazier Get up then, fathead.

Michel gets up.

Dr Piouk Who is that man?

Mlle Skunk He's a workman.

Dr Piouk (*to the glazier*) What has this got to do with you?

Glazier What has this got to do with me? (*Reflects.*) Actually, what *has* it got to do with me? (*Strokes his chin.*)

Dr Piouk Get out!

Glazier (*to Michel*) The hammer!

Mme Meck (*to Dr Piouk*) Don't provoke him, he's violent.

Michel gives the glazier the hammer.

Dr Piouk I am not afraid of anyone.

Mme Piouk Where is Victor?

Mlle Skunk He's here somewhere.

Glazier And the chisel.

Mlle Skunk (*rushing up*) Victor!

Michel gives him the chisel.

Mme Meck (*to Mlle Skunk*) What are you doing here?

Mlle Skunk That's what I'm wondering.

Mme Piouk Come and look, André.

Dr Piouk goes over to the bed.

Dr Piouk Is that Victor?

Silence. Mme Meck, Mlle Skunk, Dr and Mme Piouk surround the bed. Dr Piouk takes out his watch, bends over, takes Victor's wrist. Silence. Victor suddenly leaps up, pushes his way through the group, searches for his shoes, finds one, sticks his foot in it, searches for the other one.

Victor (*pathetically*) My shoe!

Glazier (*to Michel*) Where did you put monsieur's shoe?

Michel But *you* had it, monsieur.

Glazier (*forcefully*) Look for it!

Michel looks for the shoe, finds it, hands it to Victor, who snatches it out of his hand and goes out, one shoe on his foot, the other in his hand, comes back immediately, runs to the footlights, wants to say something but can't, makes a helpless gesture, exits, gesticulating wildly. Silence.

Such animation! (*pause*) He's left the bill behind. (*to Michel:*) Quick, take the bill and run after him. Quick!

97

Michel The bill?

Glazier (*angrily*) How old are you?

Michel Ten, Papa.

Glazier And you still don't know what a bill is?

Michel (*on the verge of tears*) No, Papa.

Glazier The account. The reckoning. The paper – there. (*He gives him a push.*) Go on! Scram!

   Michel picks up the bill and runs out.

That's my son. He's still half-witted.

Dr Piouk I'm not surprised!

Glazier Ah, you're not surprised! (*He advances on him, hammer and chisel to the fore.*)

Dr Piouk (*retreating*) Stand back! I am armed.

Mme Piouk (*running over to her husband*) André! Come on! Let's go!

Glazier (*still advancing*) Out of my way, madame.

Mme Meck This is turning into a melodrama. Are you coming, Olga?

Mme Piouk Come on, André. Don't do anything foolish!

Glazier (*changing his mind*) After all . . . who knows? . . . It may be useful . . . although I can't see how . . . (*to Dr Piouk:*) Calm down, Doctor, calm down. Are we savages? Is it anything to do with us? No. With what, then? That's what we have to try to find out. Tell me . . .

   The glazier takes Dr Piouk by the sleeve and leads him aside.

Mme Meck Olga, Marguerite, come on!

Enter **Mme Krap** *in deep mourning.*

Mme Piouk and **Mme Meck** (*in chorus*) Violette!

Mme Krap My son! Where is he?

Mlle Skunk Gone.

Mme Krap Gone?

Mlle Skunk Gone.

Mme Krap (*collapsing on to the bed*) Where?

Mlle Skunk We don't know.

Enter Michel, holding the bill.

Michel Papa!

Glazier (*to Dr Piouk*) Isn't that right? (*to Michel:*) What do *you* want?

Michel I couldn't find him, Papa.

Glazier You couldn't find him?

Michel No, Papa, I searched everywhere, Papa. It wasn't my fault, Papa.

Glazier Oh, that's enough of your Papas!

Mme Krap Who is this man?

The glazier goes and stands in front of her.

Who are you? Are you a friend of my son? What are you doing here? Why are you looking at me like that? (*She holds her hands up in front of her face. She moves her hands apart.*) Who are you?

Glazier I am the glazier, madame. Allow me to offer you my condolences.

Mme Krap Your condolences?

Glazier Yes, madame, my condolences . . . (*pause*) . . . my sincere condolences.

Mme Krap Then you know! (*pause*) Where have I seen you before?

Glazier I don't know, madame. In the street, perhaps, by chance. Or maybe you are confusing me with someone else.

Mme Meck leans over and whispers in Mme Krap's ear.

Mme Krap You think so? (*She looks at the glazier.*) Perhaps . . . yes . . . you're right . . . my goodness! (*She weeps.*)

Mme Meck Violette!

Mme Krap (*wiping her eyes; to the glazier*) You are a friend of my son.

Glazier Er . . . not yet, madame.

Mme Krap Have you seen him today?

Mme Piouk But we have all seen him, Violette.

Mme Krap Did you tell him that . . .

Mme Piouk Of course, Violette.

Mme Krap What did he say?

Silence. Dr Piouk laughs to himself.

Mme Piouk André!

Mme Krap Where is he?

Silence. Mme Krap panics.

He isn't dead?

Silence.

He is dead! He is dead!

Glazier He wasn't dead five minutes, four minutes ago. Not what the living call dead.

Mme Krap He is alive!

Glazier His heart is beating, that's for sure.

Mme Krap How was he?

Glazier Tense, madame, a little tense. He doesn't appear to enjoy company much, even that of those nearest to him.

Mme Krap And he knew that . . .

Mme Meck But of course, Violette, I told him. More tactfully than you can possibly imagine . . .

Mme Krap And . . . ?

  Silence.

Mme Meck He is ill, Violette, you mustn't judge him too harshly.

Mme Krap (*plaintively*) I thought I would find him alone. I wanted to make one last attempt. You have ruined everything!

Mme Meck It was with the best of intentions, Violette.

Mme Krap (*as before*) After yesterday I believed there was nothing more to be done. Then Henri (*she sniffs*), Henri's death, you know, I thought he might perhaps listen to me. (*pause*) I am alone, now (*she sniffs*), all alone. (*She weeps.*)

Mlle Skunk Listen, Violette, you had better go home. You're going to need all your strength for tomorrow.

Dr Piouk Go with her, Marguerite.

Mme Meck Come on, dear.

Mme Krap My son! I want my son!

Mlle Skunk Leave it to us.

Mme Krap Bring him to me!

Mme Meck Come on! (*She leads Mme Krap over to the door.*)

Mme Piouk Are you coming, André?

Dr Piouk I'll follow you, darling. (*He kisses her.*) Go with your sister, she needs you.

Mme Piouk There's nothing for you to do here.

Mme Krap Bring him back to me!

   Mmes Krap and Meck start to go out.

Dr Piouk Yes there is, darling. I'll explain later. Go on, quickly. (*He pushes her gently towards the door.*) You'll see, everything will be all right in the end. (*He pushes her gently outside.*) I'll see you very soon, darling. (*He shuts the door.*)

Glazier The time we waste with these walk-ons!

Michel (*emerging from a dark corner where the audience is supposed to have forgotten him*) Papa!

Glazier *Now* what do you want?

Michel I want to go home, Papa. I'm hungry.

Glazier Just listen to the brat. (*to Dr Piouk:*) He had ten potatoes for lunch and now he's hungry. (*to Michel:*) Aren't you ashamed of yourself?

Michel I don't feel well, Papa.

Dr Piouk He's probably got worms.

Glazier You hear? You've got worms. Come here.

Michel does so.

Show the doctor your tongue. (*pause*) Put your tongue out, shrimp!

Michel puts his tongue out, and Dr Piouk inspects it with a little torch.

Dr Piouk (*switching his torch off*) The mirror of the stomach.

Glazier Well?

Dr Piouk It's dirty, dry and yellow.

Glazier (*giving Michel some money*) Go and buy yourself a sandwich. And come back right away. You hear me?

Michel Yes, Papa. (*He starts to go out.*)

Glazier Buy two.

Michel Yes, Papa. (*Exit.*)

Glazier Ah, children!

Dr Piouk And now let's get down to business. Mademoiselle and I have things to do.

Glazier I'm at your disposal. What is it actually all about, in your opinion?

Dr Piouk What it is about, if I have properly understood the different stories told me by my wife, my sister-in-law and you, dear mademoiselle, is a psychological state which is difficult to define.

Glazier That's a good start.

Dr Piouk If you please. This young man, for reasons yet to be ascertained, seems to have lost his zest for life. He used to work . . . (*to Mlle Skunk:*) He used to write, I believe?

Mlle Skunk Yes. The critics said he would make a name for himself.

Glazier Someone must have played a dirty trick on him.

Dr Piouk Right. He used to write. He doesn't write any more. He used to associate with his family normally. He has left them and doesn't want to see them any more. He became engaged, which is normal at his age, to a ravishing young lady, yes, yes, mademoiselle, ravishing, and he refuses to see her. (*to the glazier:*) I beg your pardon?

Glazier Nothing.

Dr Piouk He used to take an interest in the inexhaustible variety of the Paris scene, in art, in the theatre, in science, in politics, in each new school of philosophy, in . . .

Glazier Come to the point.

Dr Piouk And he had become a genuine expert on the last Merovingian Kings. Had he not, mademoiselle? Right. All this is now dead for him, as if it had never existed. Am I exaggerating, dear mademoiselle?

Olga No.

Dr Piouk He used to travel, both for pleasure and to broaden his mind. But now . . .

Glazier What class?

Dr Piouk Now, for months on end, he has never left this . . . (*looks around him*) this revolting hovel. He used to have money; now . . .

Glazier OK, OK, we've got the picture.

Dr Piouk If you keep interrupting me, I shall simply be obliged to leave. Although I should like nothing better.

Glazier But you're so long-winded. Nobody is asking you for a catalogue. He doesn't do anything any more, he's not interested in anything any more, he doesn't want to see anybody any more, we know all that. What's the next step? What has to be done to get him tolerated?

Dr Piouk Get him tolerated?

Glazier But of course. It's absurd. A creature like that doesn't make sense.

Dr Piouk But to get him tolerated? By whom? No no, we must quite simply come to his aid, and, by coming to his aid, come to the aid of his family and . . .

Glazier No no, oh no, you don't understand. No one will give a toss if he croaks, on condition that . . .

Dr Piouk Monsieur, if you have anything to say – anything reasonable, that is, which I very much doubt – you can say it later, when *I* have finished. You asked my opinion. I'm giving it to you. There is no arguing about it. I never argue. I'm sorry. Am I to go on? Or am I to leave?

Mlle Skunk Go on, please go on, you're the only person who says things I can understand.

Dr Piouk Ah, mademoiselle, if only you knew, if only you knew! (*He daydreams.*)

Glazier Carry on then, she'll never know.

Dr Piouk Where had I got to?

Glazier You were raving about the necessity of coming to his aid and, by aiding him, aiding his family and, by aiding his family, aiding goodness knows who, the whole of humanity probably. You must love humanity, Doctor?

Dr Piouk You are most uncouth. No matter. Right. Yes. I was indeed saying that by aiding him I would be aiding his family, and, first and foremost, you, dear mademoiselle, who have been so incomprehensibly deserted, so pusillanimously, madly abandoned. The problem, then, amounts to this: the appropriate method of . . . how can I put it? . . . restoring him to himself and, hence, to other people.

Silence.

I have it, this method . . . (*patting his stomach*) here.

Mlle Skunk Oh Doctor, if only you could!

Dr Piouk Yes. (*He reflects.*) When I was the director . . . Isn't there a chair anywhere here?

Glazier No. He's lost interest in chairs. But there's a bed. Of all the objects that poison our existence, that's the only one he can still tolerate. Ah, beds! Sit down.

Dr Piouk (*after a glance at the bed*) No thanks. Never mind. What was I saying?

Mlle Skunk When you were the director . . .

Dr Piouk Ah yes. When I was the director of the Saint-Vitus asylum in the Haute-Marne, every day, or rather every other day, I used to see a lunatic of Romanian origin who believed himself to be suffering from . . . (*He glances at Mlle Skunk, lowers his voice.*) from syphilis. Do I need to say that he wasn't?

Glazier Of course you need to say it.

Dr Piouk Every time, in despairing tones, he asked me whether I had brought him the poison. The poison? I would say, what poison, my friend, and what for? To put an end to my torture, he would reply. But, my dear friend, if you are absolutely determined to put an end to your torture, you have everything you need at your disposal. Three times a day you eat in the refectory, surrounded by plates, cups, forks and even knives – enough to put an end to a thousand tortures. Then he would become angry, and say that it was incumbent upon me, as his doctor, and not upon him, to put an end to his torture. But what torture, actually? I would say. There is nothing the matter with you. Fourteen doctors have examined you completely independently and found nothing wrong with you. But there is, there is, he would reply, I've got . . . ahem . . . (*same business as before*) syphilis, and it's your duty to do away with me. And that was how our conversations ended, always in exactly the same way. (*pause*) Until the day when I took him the poison he demanded.

Silence.

Mlle Skunk (*panting*) And then?

Dr Piouk He recovered rapidly.

Silence.

Glazier He wasn't a real madman.

Dr Piouk I shall not waste my time arguing about that. (*pause*) What about Victor? Is he a real madman?

Silence. Suddenly Dr Piouk starts to make rather odd gestures, tries out a dance step, waves his arms around as if semaphoring – whatever suits the actor – then stands stock still. Slight embarrassment.

Yesterday I was telling the late lamented Monsieur Krap – a remarkable man, incidentally, in his own way – I was setting forth my manner of envisaging the problem of human existence, for in my opinion it *is* a problem, in spite of present-day efforts to prove the contrary. (*pause*) I might even say that I see no other problem. (*pause*) Not being an ant, for example, or a whale. (*pause*) You were there, mademoiselle?

Mlle Skunk Yes.

Dr Piouk You see, I am not inventing anything. I was saying, then, that when pestered with questions – for I do not like to put myself forward – I said that for my part I adopted the solution to this problem of consciousness which has already been suggested by numerous thinkers, and which quite simply consists in eliminating consciousness. I was saying that it was the methods of this elimination, the technical aspect, that particularly interested me, for I am a man of action, and I mentioned some of the most effective means, in my opinion, of achieving this result with the maximum promptitude and the minimum inconvenience. Do I need to add that I do not believe in them for a moment? I mean: life has cured me of all hope of seeing it come to an end, on the universal scale. At the very most, we could put the brakes on. (*pause*) But I am a consistent man, in my own way, courageous, in a sense, and, if I may say so, a man of integrity, and I hold myself at the disposal of those who, while sharing my opinion, are even more pessimistic and determined than I.

Mlle Skunk But you want to kill him!

Glazier Do you imagine that he needs you in order to put an end to himself – always supposing that that is what he really wants?

Dr Piouk My dear friend, it is amazing how much help people do need in order to cease to exist. You have no idea. One practically has to hold their hand. (*pause*) Take my Romanian, for example. Did he need me in order to put an end to his torture? Of course not. What's more, he is now a cattle dealer in Iaşy. He writes to me from time to time. A postcard. He calls me his saviour. His saviour! Ha!

Glazier It's not the same thing. He thought he was seriously ill.

Dr Piouk I don't know precisely what this young man is

complaining of. Of something more serious, I think, than a mere illness, and certainly of something more vague, also. I have been told that he enjoys excellent health. Let us suppose that he is quite simply complaining of existing, of the life syndrome. That is conceivable, isn't it? We are no longer in the nineteenth century. We know how to look things in the face. Right. I offer him the means of no longer existing, the means of passing, with the utmost ease, from the state of consciousness to the state of pure extension . . .

Mlle Skunk No! No! I won't let you!

Dr Piouk (*wildly*) . . . and at the same time I tell him that I will remain at his side to ensure that the transition takes place without a hitch. Well, my dear friends, either he discovers good reasons – because he is the cerebral type, that's obvious – to come back and sweat it out among his fellow creatures, or else . . . (*expressive gesture*) But don't worry, in all probability he is just as much of a swine as the rest of us.

   Silence. The glazier paces up and down. Olga dismayed. Dr Piouk radiant.

Mlle Skunk It's abominable! You mustn't!

Dr Piouk Mademoiselle, if I have gone rather too far, if I have not sufficiently minced my words, you must put it down to an old enthusiasm which is about to become extinguished. For me, to speak in this way is to breathe a different air, that of my youth, of my passions, of my innocence, before the black flag and the bowed head. (*emotionally*) Mademoiselle (*He takes her chin and raises it.*) look at me. Do I look like an ogre? (*He smiles horribly.*) Have confidence! I shall save him! As I saved Verolesco.

Mlle Skunk But if he takes it?

Dr Piouk What?

Mlle Skunk The . . . the . . . poison.

Dr Piouk He won't take it.

Mlle Skunk But if he wants to take it?

Dr Piouk Well, then, (*with an effort*) well, then, it's against my principles, but to please you, well then we shall stop him. You see, dear Olga – yes, allow me to call you Olga – I am ready to do anything to please you.

Mlle Skunk But what if we get there too late?

Dr Piouk (*laughing*) Anyone can see that you are out of your depth. What a lot of things that pretty head doesn't know. What a lot of nasty things! The very idea! *I* shall know at once whether he is serious or not. Even before I give him the tablet.

Mlle Skunk It's a tablet?

Dr Piouk takes a little bottle out of his waistcoat pocket, shakes a tablet into the hollow of his hand, holds it out to Mlle Skunk, who hesitates, then takes it.

Dr Piouk There.

Enter Michel. He gives the glazier a sandwich.

Glazier Have you eaten yours?

Michel Yes, Papa.

Glazier You've been gallivanting.

Michel No, Papa.

Glazier Give me the change.

Michel gives him the change, which he counts.

Right. Hold this for me. (*He gives him back the sandwich.*)

Take these, too. (*He gives him the hammer and chisel.*) Go over there and keep quiet.

Michel goes and sits on the tool box, by the window.

Mlle Skunk (*rousing herself from her contemplation of the tablet*) So that's it!

Dr Piouk takes the tablet, puts it back in the bottle and returns the bottle to his pocket.

Dr Piouk Yes, that's it, that tiny little thing, languor, lullaby, white worlds without end, the end, peace, finality. What's the time? (*He pulls out his watch.*) Five past five! (*He puts his watch back.*) Good heavens!

Mlle Skunk And what if you . . .

Glazier (*having made his decision*) Ah, I see . . . It isn't . . .

Dr Piouk (*to the glazier*) Be quiet! (*to Mlle Skunk:*) You were saying?

Mlle Skunk What if you just gave him an aspirin?

Dr Piouk (*drawing himself up*) Mademoiselle, I am only a poor devil, but I do not trifle with sedatives. No. That is not my style. Anything you like to please you, but not that.

Silence.

Glazier I'm looking at things . . .

Dr Piouk Are you going to take long?

Glazier Not so long as you.

Dr Piouk I'll give you five minutes.

Glazier I'm looking at things from a point of view that . . .

Dr Piouk One moment. If you don't mind. What is your interest in this business? I don't quite follow.

Glazier No need to bother about that.

Dr Piouk Very well. I'm listening.

Glazier . . . from a point of view that is very far removed from yours. Whether he comes back to life, as you so charmingly put it, whether he goes on stagnating here, or whether he croaks, is a matter of complete indifference to me, provided that the thing is solidly based. Do you see what I mean?

Dr Piouk I must admit . . .

Glazier There have to be reasons, for Christ's sake! Why has he renounced everything? Why this absurd life? Why agree to die? Reasons! Jesus himself had his reasons. No matter what he does, we must know more or less why. Otherwise he'll be rejected. And so will we. Who do you think you're dealing with? Aesthetes?

Dr Piouk Decidedly, I do not grasp . . .

Glazier Can't you see that we're all revolving round something that has no meaning? We have to find a meaning for it, otherwise there's no other option than to bring the curtain down.

Dr Piouk And then what? I can't see any harm in bringing the curtain down on something that has no meaning. After all, that's what usually happens. Still, I can see that that isn't the point for you. So I won't insist. I quite simply want to answer you. You want to impose a kind of justification on this . . . how shall I put it . . . this simulacrum of life, so that both the one who leads it and those whom it afflicts can be tolerated, as you so nicely put it. Is that more or less it? Right. That is what I am doing when I face the person concerned with the possibility of taking his refusal to the cleanest and most agreeable extreme. For it really is a refusal, if I understand aright.

Glazier Yes. But you reason like an ape.

Dr Piouk That is to make it easier for you to follow me. Let's see. I offer him (*He taps his waistcoat.*) my little bonbon. He refuses. Good. Why? No matter. He wants to live. That suffices. That has a meaning. Rather vague, if you like, but sufficient. We say to ourselves – I'm putting myself on your level – the poor young man! So close to succumbing! Illuminated at the last moment! On the very brink of the abyss! One of us again! No one will ask more, believe me. Or else he accepts. Which means? That he has had enough. Why? No matter. He wants to die. That suffices. It's clear. It's luminous. Existence weighs so heavily upon him that he prefers to eliminate himself from it. Everyone can understand that. We are no longer living in the Third Republic. No need to say you've got the pox. And there we are. No more complicated than that. (*to Olga:*) Are you coming?

Glazier You have a great way of simplifying things!

Dr Piouk Everything aspires either to the black or to the white. Colour is syncopation. (*Gesture of a conjuror who has brought off his trick.*)

Mlle Skunk But will he come back here?

Dr Piouk Here or elsewhere, it doesn't matter.

Mlle Skunk But he won't see you. He won't listen to you! He won't answer you!

Dr Piouk (*laughing*) You don't know me! (*pause*) Not yet. (*to the glazier:*) Good evening. (*He leads Mlle Skunk towards the door.*)

Glazier Will you be here tomorrow?

Dr Piouk (*stopping*) The earlier the better. (*He takes out his pocket diary and flicks through it.*) Let's see, this

evening . . . this evening I have an engagement . . .
tomorrow . . . tomorrow . . . we have the funeral . . .
funeral . . . lunch . . . with the widow . . . reading of the
will . . . let's see . . . tomorrow afternoon, at about three,
half past three. (*Writes.*) Will that suit you?

Mlle Skunk And if he isn't here?

Dr Piouk Well . . . well, we shall see. Right. (*to the
glazier:*) Good evening.

Mlle Skunk Good evening.

*Exeunt Mlle Skunk and Dr Piouk. Silence. The glazier
sits down on the bed, takes his head in his hands. Michel
comes out of the shadows and goes and stands in front
of him.*

Michel (*handing him the sandwich*) Eat your tartine,
Papa.

Glazier (*raising his head*) Ah yes. (*He takes the sandwich.*)
You call this a tartine? (*He separates the two slices.*) This is
a tartine, Michel. And this is another. (*He puts them
together again.*) And this is a sandwich. Have you got that?

Michel Yes, Papa.

Glazier (*his mouth full*) A sandwich is two tartines stuck
together.

Silence.

Repeat that.

Michel A sandwich is two tartines stuck together.

Glazier Good.

Silence. The glazier reflects.

Tell me, Michel.

Michel Yes, Papa.

Glazier Are you happy with me?

Michel What's happy, Papa?

Glazier How old are you?

Michel Ten, Papa.

Glazier Ten.

Silence.

And you don't know what it means – happy?

Michel No, Papa.

Glazier You know, when there's something you enjoy.
You feel good, don't you?

Michel Yes, Papa.

Glazier Well, that's more or less what it is – happy.

Silence.

So are you happy?

Michel No, Papa.

Glazier But why not?

Michel I don't know, Papa.

Glazier Is it because you don't go to school often enough?

Michel No, Papa, I don't like school.

Glazier Would you like to be playing with your friends?

Michel No, Papa, I don't like playing.

Glazier I'm not unkind to you?

Michel Oh no, Papa.

Glazier What do you like doing?

Michel I don't know.

Glazier What d'you mean, you don't know? There must be something.

Michel (*after reflection*) I like it when I'm in bed, before I go to sleep.

Glazier Why's that?

Michel I don't know, Papa.

   Silence.

Glazier Make the most of it.

Michel Yes, Papa.

   Silence.

Glazier Come and let me kiss you.

   Michel advances. The glazier kisses him.

Do you like it when I kiss you?

Michel Not much, Papa.

Glazier But why not?

Michel It prickles me.

Glazier You see, you do know why you don't like it when I kiss you.

Michel Yes, Papa.

Glazier Then tell me why you like it when you're in bed.

Michel (*after reflection*) I don't know, Papa.

   Silence.

Glazier You're still hungry.

Michel Yes, Papa.

Glazier (*giving him the sandwich*) Here, eat this.

Michel (*hesitating*) But it's yours, Papa.

Glazier (*forcefully*) Eat it!

  Silence.

Michel Aren't you hungry any more, Papa?

Glazier No.

Michel But why not?

  Silence.

Glazier I don't know, Michel.

  Silence.

CURTAIN

Act III

Next day. Late afternoon.

   Victor's room, seen from another angle. Krap family side swallowed up by the orchestra pit. Door half-open, window broken, the glazier's tools scattered all over the floor.

   Victor alone, lying down. He is asleep. The glazier in the doorway.

Victor (*in his sleep*) No . . . no . . . too high . . . rocks . . . my body . . . Papa . . . be brave . . . brave boy . . . I am brave . . . a brave boy . . . brave boy . . .

   Silence. He tosses and turns. Louder:

Fathom . . . full fathom five . . . at low tide . . . low tide . . . fathomless . . . fathomless . . . wild waves.

   Silence. Enter the glazier. He goes up to the bed.

Those . . . eyes . . . a thousand ships . . . towers . . . circumcised . . . fire . . . fire . . .

   Silence.

Glazier Towers circumcised fire fire! This is a fine state of affairs! (*He shakes Victor.*) Get up, cesspool!

   Victor wakes up with a start, sits up, dazed.

Victor (*not properly awake*) No . . . no . . . tomorrow, I . . . (*He sees the glazier.*) What?

Glazier Gone four o'clock! Four o'clock! The day's over. The sun's going down. Your father's in his grave. And here you are, wallowing in your lascivious dreams! Pig!

Victor I'm thirsty.

Glazier (*pulling the covers back*) Get up, for Christ's sake. You've got visitors.

  Victor sits on the edge of the bed. Dressed as the day before, but no jacket.

Victor I'm terribly thirsty. (*He wipes his mouth.*) Visitors?

Glazier Good thing I looked in. They'd have found you snoring.

Victor Who? Who would have found me?

Glazier Ah! That is the question!

Victor I'm leaving. (*He stands up, starts searching.*)

Glazier Let's say: a committee of enquiry. This is the third day, the great day, when all things must be made plain. An hour from now we shall know what to make of it. What are you looking for?

Victor The glass.

Glazier The glass? Here? You must be joking.

Victor (*searching*) I saw it the other day. (*He looks under the bed, sees the glass, picks it up, goes out on to the landing, comes back with the glass full of water, sits down on the bed, drains the glass at one gulp, goes out on to the landing again, comes back with the glass full again, drains it in two gulps, puts it down on the bed, stands up, searches.*)

Glazier You have a family vault, I suppose?

Victor (*searching*) What?

Glazier Top people like you, they always have a family vault.

Victor A grain of wheat discovered in a tomb will sprout after three thousand years of desiccated sleep. (*pause*) So they say. (*He searches.*)

Silence.

Glazier What's the matter with you, dancing around in circles like . . . like a soul in torment?

Victor I'm looking for my shoes.

Glazier (*also looks; after a moment*) Here's one.

He kicks it over to Victor, who sticks his foot in it.

Are you thinking of going out?

Victor (*searching*) And the other one?

Glazier (*goes and shuts the door and leans against it*) You aren't going out.

Victor I had it last night.

A knock.

Glazier Here they are.

He opens the door. Enter Jacques, with a shoe in his hand. He looks at the glazier in astonishment, makes as if to speak to him, changes his mind, advances into the room.

Jacques I hope I'm not intruding, monsieur.

Victor (*looking at the shoe*) Where did you find that?

Jacques On the stairs, monsieur. I thought I recognised monsieur's shoe.

He hands the shoe to Victor, who takes it, examines it, drops it and sticks his foot in it.

Glazier A flunkey!

Victor Are you the visitor?

Jacques doesn't understand.

Glazier With respect, monsieur, no, this is not monsieur's visitor.

Jacques Is monsieur expecting a visitor?

Victor No, I'm going out.

Jacques Did monsieur return home safely?

Victor I don't know. (*He starts searching again.*)

Jacques Is monsieur looking for something?

Victor My jacket.

Jacques helps him look for his jacket.

I've lost it. (*He goes towards the door.*)

Jacques Monsieur is not going out without a jacket?

Victor (*to the glazier*) Let me pass.

Glazier No.

Victor (*to Jacques*) Help me to get out.

Jacques Is monsieur unable to get out?

Victor He won't let me by.

Jacques (*going over to the door*) What am I to do, monsieur?

Victor Make him let me out.

Jacques (*going towards the glazier*) Remove yourself.

The glazier gives him a violent push. Jacques staggers back a few steps, stops.

Victor (*to Jacques*) Both together.

Jacques (*without enthusiasm*) As monsieur wishes. (*He advances.*)

Glazier Stop!

Jacques stops.

Did you like your master?

Victor Don't listen to him. Come on, both together.

Glazier Did he love his son?

Jacques (*wanting to please everyone*) Does that concern you?

Victor (*feebly*) Come on, one, two . . .

Glazier (*to Jacques, forcefully*) He has to stay here. For his own good. (*pause*) And, anyway, I wouldn't hesitate to knock you both out.

Silence. Victor goes and sits down on the bed. Jacques is embarrassed.

Jacques Is monsieur angry?

Silence.

I don't know what to say, monsieur. Violence is not in my line, monsieur. If monsieur will please excuse me.

Victor Of course, of course. (*pause*) What did you want?

Jacques I had something to say to monsieur. (*pause*) No one sent me. I thought . . .

Victor Tell me.

Jacques Madame, monsieur's mother . . .

Glazier Is this formality really necessary?

Victor He's right. Try and speak as if you were a human being and as if I was, too. If you don't mind.

Jacques Monsieur, your mother is ill. The funeral has been postponed.

Victor Two birds with one stone.

Jacques (*slightly scandalised*) The funeral is to be tomorrow, monsieur, at the latest.

Victor Then it isn't that.

Jacques I thought you should be informed, monsieur. Madame is in a very bad way.

Victor Is that all?

Jacques No, monsieur. Doctor Piouk was taken ill during the night. He is confined to bed.

Glazier Shit!

Victor Doctor who?

Jacques Doctor Piouk, monsieur, your aunt's husband, monsieur.

Victor My aunt's husband?

Glazier Of course, your aunt's husband. (*to Jacques:*) What's the matter with him?

Jacques I don't know exactly.

Glazier Is it serious?

Jacques I believe it is rather serious.

Victor And that's why you came? To tell me that my mother is in a very bad way, and that the husband of my aunt, whom I believed to be a virgin, was taken ill during the night?

Glazier Isn't he chatty, today!

Jacques I thought monsieur should know . . .

Glazier Hey!

Jacques . . . I thought you should know the state the family is in on the eve of the funeral.

Glazier He doesn't give a shit.

Jacques And then, I wanted to make sure that monsieur . . . that you had returned home safely last night, and also to tell you how pleased we were, Marie and I, with your kind words.

Glazier Words? Was he wording?

Jacques I don't wish to be presumptuous, but the house has never been the same since you left, monsieur Victor. Naturally, nobody told us anything, but we knew enough to form some idea of the kind of life you were leading (*circular glance*) A faint idea. We . . . I'm not boring you, monsieur?

   Silence.

I am boring you, I knew I was.

Glazier It doesn't matter. Go on.

Jacques May I go on, monsieur?

Victor (*to the glazier*) Are you going to let me by?

Glazier Get this into your head. There is only one thing I ask, and that is that you should take shape. Just the slightest glimmer of sense, enough to make people say, 'Ah, so that's what it is, now I'm beginning to understand' – and then I'll disappear.

Victor (*to Jacques*) Go on.

Jacques I don't really know how to put it. I simply felt that you didn't ought to . . .

Victor Ought not to.

Jacques . . . to be left in ignorance of how touched we were, Marie and I, by what you said to us. We would have liked to tell you so last night, but you left so abruptly.

Glazier Patience, patience.

Jacques We had so often wondered what had happened, and why you never came to the house. It made us sad to see monsieur so unhappy. We didn't want to think badly of you, you had been so good to us, and yet there were times when . . . So it really did something to us when you explained . . .

Glazier Explained? What did he explain?

Jacques (*stammering*) Well . . . he explained . . . he told us why . . . why he couldn't do anything else.

Glazier He explained that?

Jacques Yes.

Glazier And you understood?

Jacques is embarrassed.

You didn't understand a word.

Jacques That's to say . . .

Glazier Do you remember what he said?

Jacques We understood that it was serious, that it wasn't . . .

Glazier Just quote me one sentence, one single sentence.

Silence.

Wonderful! He's only prepared to explain himself off-stage, and then only to imbeciles.

Jacques It was clear at the time. It isn't a thing you can describe. It's a bit like music.

Glazier Music! (*He walks up and down in front of the door.*) What crimes! What crimes! (*He comes to a halt.*) Music! I get the picture. Life, death, liberty, the lot, and the cynical little laughs to show that one is not fooled by noble words and fathomless silences, and the gestures of the paralytic who is trying to indicate that it isn't *that*, oh, no, one says that but it isn't that at all, it's something different, something completely different, there's nothing to be done, language wasn't created to express that sort of thing. So let us have the decency to keep quiet, yes, decency, good night, let's go to bed, we were crazy to dare to talk of anything other than food restrictions. Oh, I can hear it, your music. Naturally you were all drunk.

Jacques Drunk?

Glazier He speaks. It's music. You listen to him. You understand. Then you don't understand any more. He loses his shoes. He loses his jacket. At four in the afternoon he's still snoring. He's delirious. Towers . . . circumcised . . . fire . . . fire . . . you come to see whether he returned home safely. That's clear. (*to Victor:*) I bet you don't remember a word you said.

Victor What? May I go now?

Glazier You see this creature?

Victor I don't understand.

Glazier He's a servant.

Victor But I know him.

Glazier He goes out of his way to come and thank you for the revelations you honoured him with last night, him and a certain Marie. Do you understand that?

Victor Revelations? (*to Jacques:*) Did I make any revelations to you?

126

Glazier Call it what you like. What did you say to him?

Victor But . . . I don't remember exactly. It was of no great interest.

Glazier Music of no great interest. You were all drunk, I tell you.

Jacques I assure you . . .

Glazier You don't know these exceptional characters. They only have to see a cork and they end up under the table. You are not going to make me believe that he was capable of confronting his father's corpse without some sort of stimulant.

Victor Leave my father out of this.

Glazier (*rubbing his hands*) Ah, that's the way we'll get at him!

Spectator (*standing up in a box*) Stop it! (*He steps stiffly over the front of the box and cautiously climbs down on to the stage. He advances towards the bed.*) Pardon this intrusion.

Glazier Are you a delegate?

Spectator No, not exactly. But I was in the bar, in the foyer, and I was chatting with some friends and family. I even bumped into a critic during the first interval.

Glazier Was he coming or going?

Spectator He was going.

Glazier In short, you were seeing which way the wind blew.

Spectator That's right.

Glazier And it blew you here.

Spectator If you like. But basically, I only had to use my common sense. Because I'm not just one, I'm a thousand spectators, all slightly different from each other. I've always been like that, like a bit of old blotting paper, of extremely variable porosity.

Glazier Then you never get bored.

Spectator (*earnestly*) Well, yes, I do sometimes.

Glazier And have you always been like that, like a bit of old blotting paper?

Spectator Monsieur, when I was a baby, my mother sometimes refused me her breast, she probably thought I was drinking too much. Well, I understood her!

Enter **Mme Karl**.

Mme Karl I've had enough.

Glazier Me too.

Mme Karl (*going over to the bed, to Victor*) For the last . . . (*She sees the spectator.*) Who's that?

Glazier He's the People's Commissar.

Mme Karl I didn't see him come past.

Glazier He came through the roof.

Mme Karl (*to the glazier*) You think you're a nine days' wonder, don't you?

Glazier Only *nine* days! What's this latest insinuation?

Mme Karl Ah! (*Gesture of disgust. To Victor:*) For the last time, are you staying or are you going?

Victor What?

Mme Karl (*violently*) I asked you whether you're staying or whether you're going. I've had a bellyful.

Glazier You're not the only one.

Victor Whether I'm staying or whether I'm going. (*He reflects*.) You want to know whether I'm staying or whether I'm going?

Glazier No no, you don't understand. She wants . . .

Mme Karl (*to the glazier*) Shut up! (*to Victor:*) Yesterday you were going, then you weren't going, this morning you were still going but here you still are. You've got the bill. Pay me and get out. There's two fellows after the room.

Victor You can't turn me out like that.

Mme Karl Turn you out! You were the one who wanted to leave!

Victor I believe I made a mistake.

Glazier And anyway, what sort of behaviour is this? Can't you see we're in conference? This is a historic moment, and you come butting in and boring us with tales of your wretched lodgings.

Mme Karl What do I care about your conferences?

Victor Listen, madame Karl, I shall be going out in a minute . . . (*He falls into a reverie*.)

Mme Karl I . . .

Glazier Shh! He's meditating.

   Silence.

Victor I'm going out to get some air.

Glazier How poetic! How profound!

Victor I'll tell you on my way out what I've decided.

Mme Karl And then you'll tell me on your way back that you've changed your mind.

Victor No, madame Karl, it will be a definite decision, I promise.

Mme Karl Because me, I've had enough.

Glazier What about me, then?

Mme Karl Up to here. (*She indicates the level. Exit.*)

   Silence.

Spectator The woman's right. (*pause*) What was I saying? Ah yes, my mother, yes . . .

Voice from the Box That's enough chat! Come to the point!

Glazier Obviously, it's better for it to be you rather than rotten eggs.

Spectator I'm not promising anything! (*Pulls out his watch.*) Half past ten. That's to say, this has already gone on for an hour and a half. (*He puts his watch back. To Victor:*) Do you realise?

Victor What?

Glazier Don't make matters worse.

Spectator You're right. I shall try to keep calm. And to be quick. Because time (*pulls out his watch*) is short. (*He puts his watch back.*) Sit down.

Glazier Sit down?

Spectator Of course. We're all fed up with watching you float around like autumn leaves.

Glazier But where?

Spectator On the floor, on the bed, wherever you like!

Glazier (*to Jacques*) Well, my friend, what do you say to that?

Jacques I must go.

Spectator (*vehemently*) Sit down!

The glazier – with feigned eagerness – and Jacques sit down on the bed, on either side of Victor, who is slumped down on his elbow; the glazier roughly pushes him upright. The spectator turns round to the box.

Pass me a chair, Maurice.

A chair is passed to him.

And my coat.

His coat is passed to him. He takes the chair over to the bed, facing it, puts on his coat, sits down, crosses his legs, passes his hand through his sparse hair, stands up, goes back to the box.

And my hat.

His hat is passed to him, he puts it on and goes and sits down again.

Glazier I forgot to bring my notebook.

Spectator I shall be brief. Don't interrupt me unless you're sure you're going to say something witty. We've been somewhat deprived of wit so far. (*He clears his throat.*) Right. I shall endeavour to keep it clean. This farce has . . . But I was forgetting. Before I begin . . . (*to the glazier:*) where is your son today?

Glazier He's ill.

Spectator Now there's a reply worthy of this show. I didn't ask you how he is, I asked you *where* he is.

Glazier He's at home, in bed.

Spectator And his mother?

Glazier (*threateningly*) Leave his mother out of this.

Spectator OK, OK, that's all we wanted to know.

Glazier Just as well for you.

Spectator OK. This farce . . . (*Once again he clears his throat, but this time, instead of swallowing the result, he spits it out into his handkerchief.*) This farce has gone on long enough.

Glazier My very words.

Spectator I say farce deliberately, in the hope of covering up for you. That's what our best authors do, they call their most serious works farces, in case no one is prepared to take them seriously.

Voice from the Box That's enough crap. Come to the point.

Spectator It's odd. No sooner am I on stage among you lot, than I start to dry up. To lose my resources. (*pause*) Considerable though they be. (*pause*) Everything has become hazy, blurred, I can't see properly. (*Puts his hand over his eyes.*) I don't even remember what I was saying.

Voice from the Box The farce, the farce. Gone on long enough.

The prompter comes out of his box, climbs up on to the stage, script in hand.

Prompter That's it! That's the end! You're not following the script. You make me sick. Good night. (*Exit.*)

Glazier The script! The script! Leave us the script!

Enter the script by air. It crashes down on to the ground.

Now we're in a mess!

Spectator I shall make one last effort.

Glazier Hang on! (*to Jacques and Victor:*) What are you mumbling about? (*They stop mumbling. To the spectator:*) What can anyone do with a guy like that?

Spectator I am just about to tell you. I remember now. This farce . . .

Glazier There's no need to say the same thing ten times. You aren't in the toilet with the critics, now. Get on with it.

Spectator You shouldn't keep going on about the critics. They can't put up with more than one kick in the arse per play. They aren't like deceived husbands.

Glazier Say what you have to say and let's get it over.

Spectator There's one thing I've noticed. I didn't walk out. Why not? Curiosity? If you like. Because, by definition, I am partly despicable. Or was it to find out whether you're going to manage to make him talk? If you like. Or to watch your absurd scene with the poison? I will admit that I'm just as much the simple soul who weeps at a melodrama as the cynic who refuses to be made a fool of. And then, my best friend's wife isn't free until gone eleven, and it's a bit warmer here than in the café. (*He shivers, turns up his coat collar.*) But none of that is important. No, if I'm still here, it's because there is something in this story that completely paralyses me, that stupefies me. How can I explain it? Do you play chess? No. Doesn't matter. It's like when you're watching a game of chess between two fifth-rate players. For three quarters of an hour neither of them has made a move, they're sitting there like a couple of morons, yawning over the chess board, and you're there too, even more of a moron than they are, rooted to the spot, disgusted, bored, tired, marvelling at so much stupidity. Until the moment when you can't stand it any longer. So you tell them, but do this, do this, what are you waiting for? Do this and it'll be over, we can go home to bed. It's unforgivable, it's against all the most elementary rules of polite behaviour, you don't even know the guys, but you can't help yourself, it's either that or having hysterics. That's more or less what is happening to me. *Mutatis mutandis*, of course. Do you follow me?

Glazier No. We aren't playing chess.

Spectator It's that business of the servant that finished us off. Your comic – what do you call him? (*He consults his programme.*) Victor, he pretends he wants to talk to us and then he goes and tells his life story *off-stage* to a half-wit of a lackey. No, no, there are limits.

Glazier (*to Jacques*) Don't you mind him insulting you like that?

Jacques (*nobly*) You need a servant here. Let his soul fit the part.

Glazier Wham! (*He covers his eye.*)

Spectator Such levity . . .

Glazier God, what a bore you are, you're such a bore. You don't understand the first thing about this business. You turn up here all of a twitter, your pockets bulging with solutions. But what solutions? You've been rabbiting on at us for the last ten minutes and we're still waiting for your solutions. Apart from all that stuff about chess, which doesn't make sense, you still haven't said anything that I haven't already said a hundred times myself, and a hundred times better, at that. You're just getting in our way. Do you think he's going to confide in you? Obviously he isn't, you nauseate him, you're simply one more pain in the arse, that's all. (*He stands up, suddenly furious.*) What the hell are you doing here? Just when I was on the point of getting him to come clean! Just when everything was going to work out! (*He advances.*) Fuck off! Fuck off!

134

He turns round at the sound of Victor standing up and making an awkward dash for the door. The glazier darts over, catches up with Victor, slaps his face, leads him back to the bed, sits him down by force. To Victor:

Bastard!

He raises his hand. Victor cringes.

Spectator Oh la la la la! Not like that! Not like that!

Glazier I'll give you one last chance to speak. And then I'll kick you by your arse – by your thousand arses – into the pit. With the greatest pleasure!

Spectator That would simply unleash the storm.

Glazier All right, I'll unleash the storm, then. It'll be a lot better than listening to you bleating like . . . like a season-ticket holder!

He leans furiously over Victor and shakes him.

Scum! Shitbag! Are you going to talk, for Christ's sake? Talk!

He suddenly lets go of him; Victor collapses on the bed.

Victor! (*He puts his head in his hands.*)

Spectator (*goes back to his chair, rests the tips of his fingers on it in an elegant attitude*) I shall be brief. I distinguish, in this charivari, two conflicting attitudes. I cannot distinguish them very clearly, but I can distinguish them. In the first place, (*to the glazier:*) yours, and I couldn't say whether it is moral, aesthetic, intellectual, or whether it quite simply stems from a kind of Stakhanovite mawkishness, as your premises are so vague and so muddled. And then there is the attitude of the doctor, which is much simpler . . . (*He consults his programme.*) . . . Doctor Piouk, who seems to believe, in so far as he

135

knows our language, that we try to avoid pain as necessarily and, let's be fair, as blindly as the moth tries to avoid the dark. I say conflicting attitudes, but they aren't even in conflict. Vaguely, wearily formulated, they co-exist, if we can call it existing, it's six of one and half a dozen of the other, as we don't give a single damn about either. And that is the basis on which you have the nerve to try to turn this poor wretch . . . (*programme*) this wretched Victor, into a comedy character. (*He wipes his forehead.*) But the worst is still to come. The terrible thing is that you're all the time getting within a hair's breadth of something – oh, I'm not saying it's something important, but even so it could provide us with a tolerable evening's entertainment. It comes close, very close, but it never gets there, it's awful. (*pause*) Actually, who wrote this rubbish? (*programme*) Beckett (*he says 'Béké'*), Samuel, Béké, Béké, he must be a cross between a Jew from Greenland and a peasant from the Auvergne.

Glazier Never heard of him. Seems he eats his soup with a fork.

Spectator Doesn't matter. Remainder him . . . No, but seriously, this could have amounted to something. You can imagine how it could have been if its characters had clear heads and fresh mouths, the two lives, the two principles, faith and pleasure, faith in no matter what and the minimum of displeasure, and the poor wretch who doesn't want either but who knocks himself out searching for something different. That would have given us a good laugh. But nothing doing.

Glazier So you like nice straightforward situations, ridiculous, hilarious ones?

Spectator Don't you?

Glazier Oh, me. Personally, you know, I don't ask much

any more. My demands get less and less. Give me the most ordinary lamp-post, just so as to draw attention to the fog, and I'll happily return to nothingness.

Spectator Listen. Let's forget about what doesn't exist, and can't exist unless we start all over again from the beginning. And let's see things as they are. Do you want . . .

Glazier Let's see things as they are, indeed! Blah, blah, blah!

Spectator Do you want him to talk, yes or no?

Glazier Well now, that's an idea! I hadn't thought of that.

Spectator Do you want him to tell us something of what he said last night to that idiotic music-lover? What d'you think of that?

Glazier What a brilliant idea. (*He turns round politely to Victor, raising his beret.*) Excuse me, monsieur. (*He taps him on the shoulder.*) Excuse me, monsieur, forgive me for interrupting your conversation, but if you would be good enough to give us a summary of your last night's declarations, made off-stage under the influence of alcohol, you would be doing us a great favour. (*becoming more and more humble and affectionate*) An enormous favour!

Spectator You're going about it like a half-wit.

Glazier (*falling on his knees, joining his hands*) Monsieur! Monsieur! I entreat you! Have pity, have pity on those who dwell in the thick darkness. (*He listens ostentatiously.*) Silence! It's like the eternal silence of Pascal's infinite spaces. (*He stands up despondently, dusts off the knees of his trousers. To the spectator:*) You see. (*He reflects.*) I'm going. You'll take my place, won't you? With him, and with (*gesture towards the audience*) them. Thank you in advance.

137

Spectator You're crazy! Can you possibly have forgotten? Or not noticed? It's staring you in the face!

Glazier I'm going home. To Crèvecoeur-sur-Auge. Good night, all. (*He starts to go out.*)

Spectator (*with such force that he begins to cough*) He's afraid of getting hurt!

The glazier turns round. A coughing fit.

He told you so himself! Idiot! The only positive statement he let slip!

Glazier You're exaggerating.

Spectator His one mistake – and you aren't taking advantage of it! (*He coughs frantically.*)

Glazier Has something gone down the wrong way?

Spectator (*becoming calmer*) You're going to tell me that it's no good, that it's too late, that the game is lost. Could be. It doesn't matter. At the stage you've got to, it's your only hope. You're going to tell me that what people say under duress doesn't count as evidence. But it does, it does. Whatever they say, they give themselves away.

Mme Piouk comes rushing in.

Mme Piouk André! André!

Jacques stands up.

My husband. Have you seen my husband?

Glazier (*to the spectator*) Have you seen her husband? No? Me neither. (*He looks under the bed.*) He's not here, madame.

Mme Piouk Hasn't he been here?

Spectator No, madame. We were waiting for him. Not

without impatience, even, but then we were told that he was taken ill during the night. A liver attack, no doubt? Well, it doesn't matter what sort – an attack of something or other. During the night. So we concluded that he wouldn't turn up. (*To the glazier:*) Didn't we?

Glazier I came to that very same conclusion.

Mme Piouk Yes, yes. He is very ill. He ought to be in bed, with ice bags on his forehead and his . . . his stomach. I left the room for a moment (*She wrings her hands.*) wretched woman that I am, but I had no choice, and when I got back he wasn't there! He had escaped! Half-undressed! Without a hat! (*Sobs.*) André! Without a hat! I knew he was supposed to come here this afternoon. So I took a taxi. And he isn't here!

Glazier What a family!

Spectator (*politely*) But you have probably quite simply arrived ahead of him, madame. Wait a little while. He won't be long.

Mme Piouk But he doesn't know what he's doing any more! It's terrible!

Spectator (*shocked*) He doesn't know what he's doing?

Glazier Have you been to your sister's, madame?

Mme Piouk To Violette's? No. Why? Do you think he could have gone there?

Glazier Seeing that he doesn't know what he's doing. (*pause*) Maybe he wanted to enquire after her health.

Mme Piouk But he didn't even know . . . yes, though, he did know she was ill. I told him last night. But he must have forgotten. He had forgotten everything. He didn't even recognise me.

139

Spectator If he's forgotten everything, there's not much chance of his coming here. Just think for a moment, dear madame.

Mme Piouk But he might suddenly have remembered everything.

The glazier laughs hysterically. He walks up and down making wild gestures.

What can we do?

This passage comes to an abrupt end, as if overcome by a feeling of fatigue and fatuity. Silence. Gestures of helplessness, of indifference. Shrugged shoulders. Even Jacques, who almost said, 'Should madame perhaps inform the police?' raises his arms and lets them drop limply. Mme Piouk is prostrated. She goes over to the door, hesitates, turns round, is about to speak, changes her mind, goes out. Presentiment that the whole play could finish in the same way.

Jacques Let me leave.

Glazier (*to the spectator*) We don't need him any more, do we?

Spectator I don't.

Glazier (*to Jacques*) Then you may go.

Jacques (*to Victor*) Does monsieur desire anything?

Glazier Go, go, go. Monsieur has no desires. Scram.

Jacques hesitates, looks sadly at Victor, raises his arms and goes out.

Spectator Come on, then. One last effort.

Glazier You think so?

Victor I'm thirsty.

Spectator What did he say?

Glazier That he's thirsty. (*pause*) I can't remember where we'd got to. All these interruptions.

Spectator He's afraid of getting hurt.

Glazier Ah yes. Maybe he was lying.

Spectator We shall see.

Glazier We can't torture him.

Spectator Why not?

Glazier It's not done.

Spectator Since when?

Glazier I couldn't.

Spectator Nor could I.

Glazier So?

Spectator You'll see. (*He turns round to the box.*) Chouchi! Come down here.

Chouchi comes down on to the stage and advances with a broad oriental smile.

You've got the picture?

The smile grows broader.

Have you got the pincers?

Chouchi displays the pincers. To the glazier:

Tell him.

Glazier Victor! (*He shakes him.*) You *must* talk, now.

Victor What?

Glazier You *must* explain yourself.

Victor Explain what? I don't understand. Go away.

At a gesture from the spectator, Chouchi advances.

Glazier (*to the spectator*) Is he a Taoist?

Spectator A staunch Taoist.

Glazier Aïe!

Chouchi advances.

Victor! Wake up! This time it's serious. They're going to pull your nails out. (*to Chouchi:*) Aren't you?

Chouchi Jlust a flew nlails flirst.

Glazier (*to Victor*) You hear? Just a few nails first.

Victor raises his head, sees the Chinese, the smile, the pincers, recoils in terror.

Spectator He understands.

Glazier (*holding Victor firmly*) Talk!

Chouchi advances.

Victor (*in a panic*) What? Talk about what? I don't know how to talk! What do you want with me? Killers!

Spectator (*to the glazier*) Ask him some questions.

Glazier Tell us what you told Jacques.

Victor But I didn't tell him anything! I don't remember! I forget! What have you all got against me? I haven't done you any harm! Leave me alone!

Spectator That's a bit vague. But at least something's beginning to trickle out. (*to Chouchi:*) Incidentally, have you got the catheter?

Chouchi brings one out of his pocket and displays it. Smile.

Glazier It's true that he hasn't done us any harm.

Spectator His mistake was not to know how to conceal himself. Ask him some questions.

Glazier Why did you leave your family? Your fiancée? Your pleasures? Your work? Why are you leading this kind of life? What is your aim? What are your intentions?

Victor I don't know, I don't know.

Spectator You're asking him too many questions at once.

Glazier Why are you leading this kind of life? No, that's not it. In the first place, what kind of a life is it that you've been leading for over two years? What . . .

Spectator That's enough. Chouchi.

> *Signals to him to advance. Chouchi does so. So does the spectator. They halt in front of Victor.*

Did you hear the question? What kind of a life is it that you've been leading?

> *Movement of pincers.*

Glazier Quick, say something! Anything. We'll help you.

Victor I'll try.

Glazier Bravo! (*to the spectator and Chouchi:*) Stand back! Give him air.

> *The spectator and Chouchi step back.*

Victor It won't be the truth.

Glazier So what.

Victor It'll be boring.

Glazier That's a more serious matter.

Victor You'll have asked for it.

Glazier Quite correct.

Silence.

Shh! He's going to take the plunge.

Victor When I was a little boy . . .

Spectator For God's sake, spare us the background history, we haven't got all night. Stick to the question.

Glazier Victor interrupted! Now we've seen everything!

Victor You find my way of life sordid and incomprehensible. It would be natural if you were to turn away from it in disgust. But what do you do? You never stop prying into it. You can't tear yourselves away from it. You keep prowling around it. Nothing puts you off. And when night separates us, you think about me.

Spectator That's because you've come into the public domain.

Victor I obsess you. Why? Ask yourselves. It isn't me you should be interrogating, it's yourselves.

Glazier It's true that he doesn't know how to talk.

Victor My family, my fiancée, my friends, it may be normal – what's called normal – for them to persecute me. But you? You're strangers. I don't know you. What can it matter to you how I live? And you are not the first. Ever since I've been living like this – for two years now, so you say – I've been pursued by people I don't know.

Glazier They want to understand. You provoke them.

Victor But why this sudden mania to understand a life like mine? You come across an infinite number of mysteries every day, and you pass by on the other side. But with me you stop and stare, hypnotised, hungry for knowledge, basely curious, determined to see through me.

144

Silence.

You're jealous!

Silence.

Saints, madmen, martyrs, victims of torture – they don't bother you in the least, they are in the natural order of things. They are strangers, you will never be one of them, at least you hope you won't. You are not jealous of them. You turn away from them. You don't want to think about them. They fill you with horror and pity.

Silence.

Faced with a solution which is not that of death, you are filled with horror and pity! And with relief, too. You are at ease. It's not worth worrying about. Nothing to do with you. If such people are far removed from your own distress, yet perhaps suffering from another – although inconceivable – kind of distress, they have certainly paid the price. Nothing wrong with that, then. The books balance.

Glazier What eloquence!

Victor May I stop, now?

Spectator Stop! But you haven't said anything worth saying, yet. Just forget your generalisations, if you please. It's your particular case we are concerned with, not that of the human race.

Victor But they are interdependent.

Spectator What? Balderdash! And, anyway, talk a bit louder, we can't hear you.

Silence.

Get a move on!

Glazier Give him time. The house isn't on fire.

Spectator Time! Do you know what time it is? (*He pulls out his watch.*) Eleven o'clock! (*He puts his watch back.*) Gone eleven.

Glazier You're six hours fast.

Spectator Very funny. We ask him a nice simple question: What kind of a life is it that you're leading? And he replies with an avalanche of absurdities about *our* life and the life of the insane. He'd better answer the question, or I shall take drastic steps.

Glazier (*to the spectator*) Any minute now I'm going to smash your face in.

Victor The kind of life I lead? It's the life of someone who doesn't want to lead your kind of life – oh, I'm not talking about yours in particular, no one would want that, but of the life that is yours in the sense that there's only a difference of degree between you and what they call real living beings. But whether it's that higher life, or yours, or the others', I want nothing to do with it; because I've got it into my head that, at whatever level, it's always the same old grind.

Spectator But you are alive. You can't deny that. In what way is your life different from ours? There's an apparent difference. But basically?

Victor Do you really think I'm alive? Are you stooping so low as to compare yourself with me? You might perhaps have some fellow-feeling for the poorest of the poor, but not for me. Would you be so dead set on understanding me, on accounting for me, on leading me back to the fold, if you felt I was really one of you? No, because in that case there wouldn't be anything to understand. A passing look of pity, or disgust, or even of anger, and that would be the end of it, you'd think no more about it. But you feel there is something else, that my life is essentially different from

146

yours, that there is a gap between you and me just as there is a gap between you and the mad, only it's not the same gap. In the case of the madman, you accept it. But in my case, you don't. Why not? Unless I too am mad. But you don't dare hope for that.

Glazier Talk about boring!

Spectator You are asked what kind of a life it is that you're leading. You tell us all about what it isn't. Excuse me, I hope I haven't offended you: you tell us a little about what it isn't. That's what's called negative anthropology. At the same time you inform us of our feelings about you. We know them better than you do. If you are really incapable of answering the question, say so, I'll get someone to give you a helping hand.

Victor It's a life . . .

Spectator Excuse me. Just a moment. Are you now talking about *your* life? And not about ours, or the life of the bees?

Victor About mine.

Spectator Marvellous!

Victor It's a life consumed by its own liberty.

Glazier Why don't we kill him, then? How would that be for a curtain?

Spectator Let's wait a bit longer. (*to Victor:*) Go on.

Victor It won't take long. I have always wanted to be free. I don't know why. Nor do I know what it means, to be free. If you were to pull all my nails out, I wouldn't be able to tell you. But although I can't put it in words, I do know what it is. I have always desired it. I still desire it. That is all I desire. At first I was a prisoner of other people. So I left them. Then I was a prisoner of myself. That was worse. So I left myself. (*Becomes absent.*)

147

Silence.

Spectator But this is fascinating. How does one leave oneself?

Victor What?

Spectator I said this is fascinating. Go on. Just tell us what you have to do to leave yourself.

Victor (*incoherently*) You accept it when someone is beyond life, or when life is beyond you, and that people can refuse to compromise with life if they are prepared to pay the price and give up their liberty. He's abdicated, he's dead, he's mad, he's got faith, got cancer. Nothing wrong with that. But not to be one of you through being free, that's a disgrace and a scandal. Then it's the furious hatred old maids feel for whores. Your own liberty is so miserable! So paltry! So threadbare! So ugly! So false! And you value it so enormously! You never mention it. Ah, envious, you're envious! (*Takes his head in his hands.*)

Glazier Well, now we know!

Spectator Know? What do we know? Do we know ourselves? (*to Victor:*) Pull yourself together.

Victor (*raising his head*) I've no more to say to you.

Spectator Oh yes you have! You have! You have to tell us how you go about leaving yourself. That is what particularly interests my friends.

Victor To hell with your friends!

Spectator Chouchi.

Chouchi advances.

Victor Can you really take account of what I say under constraint? Are you as screwed up as that?

Spectator We have already settled that question. In your absence. And anyway, you only have to see the result. What you have said makes sense. It's a bit primitive, maybe, a bit naïve, but it makes sense. We don't ask any more. Our demands are modest, contrary to what you seem to imagine. (*to the glazier:*) Aren't they?

Glazier Sod off.

Spectator (*to Victor*) You left yourself. That's the latest twist in your serial story. How did you go about it?

Victor By being the least possible. By not moving, not thinking, not dreaming, not speaking, not listening, not perceiving, not knowing, not wishing, not being able, and so on. I believed that that was where my prisons lay.

Glazier I believe I'm going to be sick.

Spectator (*to Victor*) Ah, you believed. And did you succeed in not moving, not gabbing, and all the rest of it? Even so, you must have had a bite to eat from time to time, I suppose, during those two heroic years. It must have been a bit difficult, sometimes, to keep yourself uncontaminated by any kind of ideation. And you went out in your sleep, like an owl at night. Not to speak of the visits inflicted on you, which you probably must sometimes have been aware of, in spite of yourself.

Victor It takes patience.

Spectator Obviously, obviously; everything is difficult at first. But even so, you do now feel yourself a little less . . . er . . . a little less of a captive?

Victor I think I'm on the right road.

Spectator And death. Death, full stop. Doesn't that appeal to you?

Victor If I was dead, I wouldn't know I was dead. That's the only thing I have against death. I want to enjoy my death. That's where liberty lies: to see oneself dead.

Silence. The glazier turns away and hiccups into his handkerchief.

Glazier (*wiping his mouth*) I consider this discussion closed. The essentials have been said.

Spectator I agree with you. We all have our own little point of departure, now. To take things any further would be to go back into the fog.

Victor You know that what I have told you isn't the truth?

Spectator The truth! (*to the glazier:*) Did you hear him? He's terrific! (*to Victor:*) We know it, monsieur, we know it, don't bother your head about that. When we want the truth we apply elsewhere, everyone has his own purveyor. No, don't you worry about that. And anyway, you don't know what truth is. Nor do we. You may have told it without knowing. And without us knowing.

Victor I told you a story to get you to leave me in peace.

Spectator If you like, if you like. Perhaps less than you think. Stories don't get told with impunity. In any case, we aren't asking any more from you. It wasn't at all bad, your story, a bit long, a bit boring, a bit . . . stupid, but not bad, not bad at all, even quite nice in places, provided we don't look at it too closely, which is a thing we never do. I congratulate you, I thank you, and I will now withdraw.

Victor I have something else to say.

Glazier He's crazy. You give them a finger and they take an arm.

Spectator No, no, believe me, don't say any more, you'll ruin everything.

Victor Three words.

Spectator (*magnanimous*) All right, three words, if you absolutely insist, but no more.

Victor I'm giving up.

  Silence.

Spectator You're giving up?

Glazier Don't do that, don't say that. Just when everything's settled.

Victor I'm giving up being free. No one can be free. I was wrong. I can't go on living this kind of life. I understood that last night, when I saw my father. No one can see himself dead. That's histrionics. I can't . . .

Spectator Hang on, hang on, let me think! (*He thinks.*) This changes everything. (*to the glazier:*) What do you say?

Glazier I say shit. (*pause*) And double shit.

Spectator After all, why not? Maybe it's better like that. (*to Victor:*) And what do you intend to do, in that case? What is there for you to do now?

Victor I don't know.

Glazier (*groaning*) Here we go again.

Spectator You can't continue like this?

Victor No, I can't.

Spectator It's beyond you?

Victor Yes.

Spectator Well then, be logical. Either it's life, with all the . . . all the . . . subjection it entails, or it's . . . the great departure, the real one, to use one of the metaphors you're so fond of. Isn't it?

Victor I don't know.

Spectator Oh come on!

Glazier He can drop dead, now. We know why. Let's get out of here.

Spectator Or he can go back to his family, revive his mother, bury his father, come into his inheritance, satisfy his fiancée, found a review, a church, a family, a film club, God knows what. Dead or alive, he belongs to us, he's one of us again. That's all we had to prove. That basically there's only us. It's even much better this way. It's more decent. (*to Victor:*) Thanks. (*He goes up to him, holding out his hand.*) My brother!

Victor doesn't take his hand; perhaps he doesn't see it.

No? It doesn't matter. Of no importance. Simple question of taste. Good night. Come on, Chouchi.

He goes towards the box, followed by Chouchi, still smiling in spite of everything.

Glazier That way (*pointing to the wings*).

Spectator Why?

Glazier That way, I tell you.

He advances threateningly. The spectator turns and faces him. Chouchi also.

Do you think I'm afraid of your Pekinese? (*He advances.*)

Spectator Your attitude amazes me. I get you out of trouble and you threaten me with violence.

Victor What does it matter which way he goes? Now that the harm has been done.

Spectator The harm! So that's the thanks I get!

152

Glazier Abortionist! Baboon!

He advances. The spectator and Chouchi retreat towards the wings.

Grocer!

Exeunt, briskly, the spectator and Chouchi. The glazier picks up the chair and hurls it after them, into the wings. Loud crash.

Bastard! (*He goes back to Victor.*) He's had us! (*He sees the prompter's script on the floor, picks it up and flings it into the wings.*) Bloody thing! (*He walks up and down, furious. He stops in front of Victor.*) Couldn't you have told us that a couple of hours ago, a couple of years ago? (*pause*) Ham actor! (*He walks up and down again.*) What a farce, though! (*He stops by his tools, scattered all over the floor, contemplates them with disgust.*) Just look at that!

Victor Go on giving me hell.

Glazier I haven't got the heart to pick them up. (*He turns them over idly with his foot.*) I'd have liked to take the diamond. (*He looks for it.*) So what.

Victor stands up and goes and helps him look for the diamond.

What are you doing?

Victor I'm looking for the diamond. (*He too turns the tools over with his foot.*) Maybe your son has it.

Glazier My son? You think so? He may have.

Victor It's not here.

Glazier I don't know.

Victor Are you going to leave the window like that?

Glazier Yes.

Victor And the door?

Glazier I'm going to leave it like that.

Victor Are you coming back tomorrow?

Glazier No.

Victor Take your things, then.

Glazier You can have them.

Victor You've done a good job.

Glazier Yes.

  Silence.

I ought not to have woken you up. (*pause*) Were you dreaming?

Victor Yes.

Glazier What of?

Victor I was dreaming about my father. He was . . .

Glazier No, no, don't tell me, I can't stand hearing people's dreams.

Victor He was in the water and I was on the diving board. It was . . .

Glazier Don't tell me!

Victor There were a lot of rocks in the water. He told me to dive.

Glazier To dive?

Victor But I didn't want to.

Glazier Why not?

Victor I was afraid of hurting myself. I was afraid of the rocks. I was afraid of drowning. I couldn't swim.

Glazier He would have saved you.

Victor That's what he said.

Glazier But you did dive.

Silence.

Victor I'm always having that dream.

Silence.

Did you know that character?

Glazier What character? Oh, that one. The thousand-arsed character. (*He reflects.*) I'm not angry any more. Why's that?

Victor Who is he?

Glazier What? Ah yes. I don't know. Bezique, billiards, good substantial meals, pain in the caecum, love on Saturday after the show, partiality for clarity, moderation in all things. (*He listens.*) There's someone on the landing. (*He half opens the door cautiously, looks out of it. Silence. He shuts the door cautiously.*) Well I never! (*He rubs his hands.*) Well well, that's a nice surprise. I'd given him up.

Victor Who is it?

Glazier It's the king of Catalysis and his girlfriend. It'll take them quite a while yet. (*He reflects.*) Don't you want to see this crap through to the end?

Victor I don't understand.

Glazier And tell us what you've decided?

The door half opens, the glazier runs over and shuts it. Through the door:

Just a moment! We'll call you. Have another little cuddle! Until something better comes along! (*to Victor:*) Of course.

What you've decided, in the final stage of the Dupont dilemma?

Victor I haven't decided anything.

Glazier Except that you can't carry on like this. Well then? Gee up! Just one more tiny little effort. The last. To please me.

Victor I tell you I don't know. Don't you think this massacre has gone far enough?

Glazier Just one more tiny little corpse. What harm can that do you? At the point you've got to?

Victor I don't know.

Glazier I don't know! I don't know! Is anyone asking you to know? (*The door half opens again, the glazier shuts it. Through the door:*) Just a moment! (*to Victor:*) Say something. Anything. Do you want to go back to the boogie-woogie set? Shit! Do you or don't you?

Victor smiles.

You smile? You dare smile!

He opens the door. Enter Mlle Skunk and Dr Piouk, imperfectly dressed.

Dr Piouk Still playing practical jokes.

Mlle Skunk Victor! (*She throws herself into his arms. Awkward process.*)

Glazier (*flapping his arms like a butterfly*) From flower to flower, from object to object.

Dr Piouk To work! My time is limited. Why are you still in the dark?

Glazier Well, old bodice-ripper, where've you been? Your concubine has been looking for you everywhere.

Mlle Skunk (*moving away from the bed*) He's in a sweat! (*to the glazier:*) Have you told him?

Dr Piouk Light.

Glazier How is his mother?

Mlle Skunk In a very bad way. Have you told him?

Glazier (*to Victor*) Did you hear? Mama is at death's door.

Victor stands up, wanders vaguely round the bed. All look at him in silence. He moves towards them.

He's lost his jacket.

Dr Piouk (*singing and dancing*)
He lost his trews
While dancing to the blues.

Victor gives Mlle Skunk a questioning look, indicating Dr Piouk.

Mlle Skunk But he's Marguerite's husband, for goodness' sake.

Dr Piouk Allow me to introduce myself. Doctor André Piouk, psychopath.

Glazier And sociologist.

Dr Piouk At your service. Light.

Glazier Before we go any further . . .

Dr Piouk Light.

Glazier In a moment, in a moment. Yes, I have some good news, some great news for you. (*pause*) A lot of things have happened here this afternoon. Amazing things. What a pity you were not able to be present. But you had better things to do, no doubt. (*pause*) Do you remember last night's shemozzle? Well, everything has been sorted out, a bit here, a bit there, and bit by bit it all got wrapped up, tied up, nicely labelled, even a postman wouldn't have been able to take it to the wrong address. As for your fiancé, mademoiselle, he was positively brilliant. The report he gave us (*gesture*) – he might have been the chairman of a board of directors. A real treat. I should add that we were seconded by a suburban sub-Socrates. Honour where honour is due. Without him, I'm not sure we would have made it. (*to Victor:*) What do *you* think?

Mlle Skunk What about the great news?

Glazier Ah, yes, the great news. Well . . . would you believe it . . . no, he must tell you himself. This is a sacred moment. My mouth would profane it.

Mlle Skunk (*to Victor*) Well?

Victor Are you still listening to this joker?

Glazier That's all the thanks I get?

Mlle Skunk Isn't it true, then?

Dr Piouk What I said to her, verbatim, was: 'Dear Olga, my dear little Olga, do you want me to help you? To give him back to you? Safe and sound? Into your lovely arms? Well, then, dear Olga?' (*pause*) She understood.

Glazier (*to Victor*) Did you hear that? Her most precious possession! So that you can live! Monster!

Dr Piouk It was quite nice. (*He scratches his head thoughtfully.*) But no more.

Mlle Skunk They read the will. There's nothing in it for you. You aren't mentioned.

Glazier Vengeance! Vengeance!

Dr Piouk Marguerite is rather like . . . (*He cudgels his brains*.) . . . like raffia.

Glazier (*to Mlle Skunk*) You're very calm.

Mlle Skunk Oh, there's nothing to worry about. It's all settled. You didn't tell him?

Glazier We know the reasons for his behaviour, now. They escape me for the moment, but I'm sure I could piece them together if you're interested. (*pause*) We also know the goal he has been pursuing for the last two years. He defined it in unforgettable terms – and yet I've forgotten them. (*pause*) And we know . . . (*to Dr Piouk, who is muttering and can't keep still:*) Silence! . . . We also know . . . would you believe it . . . hold tight . . . Are you prepared for a shock? . . . We know . . . (*pause*) that he is no longer pursuing that goal.

 Silence.

What a triumph! (*violently*) But don't you understand?

Mlle Skunk Not very well.

Glazier But you're as thick as a brick!

Mlle Skunk I'm tired.

Dr Piouk But not satiated. Classic memory.

Glazier He's giving up! It's over! He's beaten! He was wrong! On the ropes! Buggered! KO! He confesses! Ask him.

Mlle Skunk Is it true, Victor? Oh, say it's true!

Glazier He saw his father last night. That finished him. I always said that that was the way we'd get at him.

Mlle Skunk Victor! My love! Is it over? Are you buggered? Oh, how wonderful!

Victor What?

Mlle Skunk You don't want to live like this any longer? Say it's really true!

Dr Piouk Silence. Enough. No more! To work! Give and take! Light!

> *The glazier switches the light on. Dr Piouk goes over to Victor, looks at him closely.*

Funny sort of face.

Mlle Skunk Perhaps now . . .

Dr Piouk Silence! Silence when I'm working! (*to Victor:*) Monsieur, I shall be brief. You don't want to live. Do you wish to die? (*He raises his hand.*) Think about it.

Victor What's it got to do with you?

Dr Piouk Be natural. Don't be afraid. Relax. This is a unique opportunity.

Victor Who told you I didn't want to live? What do you know about it? What do you call *this* (*he advances a trembling hand*) – the wind in the reeds?

Dr Piouk Monsieur, I entered your sinister family through the game of marriage. Funny sort of game. Throughout the forty-eight hours I have been in the metropolis, no one has talked of anything but you. Total nonsense. I listen. I draw my conclusions. I see only one thing: distress. I come quickly. I see you. An intelligent young man, hyper-sensitive, great independence of character, robust health – well, no lesions – incapable of prevarication, trying to find his way. Manifestations of life reduced to the minimum. With what aim? That doesn't interest me. I can see the tendency, the movement. What is its nature? (*pause*) Monsieur, a man like you, until he has three grammes of morphine in his hand, is just whistling in the dark. (*pause*)

You reject my terms? No! The purest act of consciousness, the most sublime flight of fancy, is physical. (*He takes his head in his hands.*) Makes you want to scream. You know it as well as I do, it's written in your blackheads. (*pause*) It's strictly painless, you'll see, you won't feel a moment's discomfort.

Victor I don't see what interest . . .

Dr Piouk Do you really want to know? Such a trifle? No, you are avoiding the issue. Quite simply. Listen to me. Men . . . (*He turns towards the audience, clears his throat, speaks like an announcer.*) A few personal impressions of Man. Ahem! At the very top there is the hair. That's the end, he doesn't go any farther. Another thing: his condition is repugnant to him – more or less. It's both too much and too little. But he resigns himself to it, because he carries resignation within him, the resignation of the dawn of time – that audacious ellipse! If only he had left it at that, and submitted to his condition! Oh no, though. He speaks well of it! He extols its virtues! He projects it into outer space! He leaves it with regret! Ah, the swine! He finally prefers himself to the moles and the moss! It's nauseating! (*pause*) And, to conclude, a thing I have often observed, he procreates! For the sake of procreating! (*He grasps his head*). He procreates! For the sake of procreating! (*To Victor, passionately:*) Don't be like them! Don't let yourself be taken advantage of! Don't be like so many other young hopefuls, who let themselves fade away, fade away and disappear. Taken a wrong turning? What of it? Come on! The great refusal, not the lesser one, the great one, the one that only man is capable of, the most glorious one he is capable of, the refusal of Existence! (*Wipes his forehead.*)

Mlle Skunk Calm down, calm down.

Glazier My goodness, he's getting carried away! What a gift of the gab! You'd think he was working on commission.

Dr Piouk (*searches his pocket, brings out a tablet, holds it up for a moment between thumb and first finger*) Liberty!

Glazier The sod! He always finds the right words.

Dr Piouk Take it!

He holds the tablet out to Victor, who takes it, stands up, goes over to the light. Mlle Skunk follows him anxiously.

Mlle Skunk (*to Doctor Piouk, who hasn't budged*) Doctor!

Glazier Careful!

Victor (*reading*) 'Rhône aspirin.' Do you take me for a moron?

Dr Piouk (*rushing up*) What? (*He snatches the tablet back and examines it.*) He's right! What a birdbrain! (*He slaps his head.*) That one's for me. (*He swallows it.*) Old people, cowards, bastards, the corrupt, the defeated – aspirins are for them. But for *you* . . . (*he searches in his pocket*) for you, the young, the pure, the young men of the future . . . (*he brings out the tablet, the right one*) we have something different . . . (*he displays it*) something completely different! . . . Allow me. (*He takes Victor's hand and deposits the tablet in it.*) Adorable moment! This hand – so warm, so alive! (*solicitously*) Have you got a fever?

Victor (*looking at the tablet*) Do you swallow it?

Dr Piouk It is not a suppository, monsieur.

Glazier Careful! Careful!

Mlle Skunk Victor! Give that to me!

Dr Piouk With a little cold water, if possible.

Victor What guarantee?

Dr Piouk Of what?

Victor Of efficacy.

Dr Piouk The word of a professional, monsieur, and of a gentleman. Look at me!

   Victor looks at him.

You see this eye? There's your guarantee.

Victor I believe you.

Dr Piouk Thank you.

Victor This could cost you dear.

Dr Piouk What do you care?

Victor I don't, obviously. I'm just trying to understand.

Glazier Him too! What a mess!

Dr Piouk (*angrily*) Ah, you're all the same. Give it back to me. (*He holds out his hand.*)

Victor I'll keep it. I'm going to think it over. (*pause*) No, I'll be frank with you. I have already thought it over. I don't need it. I shall keep it, though.

Glazier So there you have it. Congratulations all round. (*to Mlle Skunk:*) Now you're happy. You only have to get hold of it when he's asleep, drugged with sleep, and flush it down the toilet, with all the rest.

Dr Piouk I disgust myself. (*pause*) Profoundly.

Glazier Me too, you disgust me.

Mlle Skunk (*taking Victor by the arm*) Come away!

Glazier So calm! So self-assured!

Dr Piouk She's just that little bit frigid.

Victor 'Come away'? Where?

Mlle Skunk (*in exultation*) With me! Towards life! Hand in hand! Dawn is breaking!

Glazier Our revels now are ended. You don't want any phoney medical consolations. Go away, then! With her, since she's here. You can go a bit of the way with her.

Dr Piouk Marry her! Impregnate her! Take your pleasure, go into a trance, remember, laugh yourself sick, drop dead!

Victor There's some mistake. I'm staying here.

Silence.

Mlle Skunk But . . .

Victor (*speaking jerkily*) I've changed my mind.

Silence.

Two years isn't enough. (*pause*) A lifetime isn't enough. (*pause*) My life will be long and horrible. (*pause*) But not so horrible as yours. (*pause*) I shall never be free. (*pause*) But I shall always feel that I am becoming free. (*pause*) I'll tell you how I'm going to spend the rest of my life: I shall rub my chains one against the other. From morning to night and from night to morning. That useless little sound will be my life. I don't say my joy. I'll leave that to you — joy. My peace and quiet. My limbo. (*pause*) And you come and talk to me about love, about reason, about death! (*pause*) No! Just get out of here, get out!

Dr Piouk What was all that about? (*to Mlle Skunk:*) Would you like me to certify him?

Glazier Well, that puts the whole thing in a nutshell! (*pause*) I can't remember what I wanted, but I wouldn't be surprised to find that I've got it.

Mlle Skunk It's all over.

Glazier (*worried, to Victor*) You aren't going to mess us about and change your mind again, are you?

Victor What?

Dr Piouk It's schizophrenia.

Mlle Skunk Let's go.

Glazier You're right, he's well away.

Mlle Skunk (*to the glazier*) Do you think he might change his mind again?

Glazier I don't think so. But I'm always wrong. (*to Victor:*) Will you let her know if you change your mind again?

   Silence. The glazier takes Victor by the arm.

Will you?

Victor What's that?

Glazier Will you let the young lady know if you change your mind again?

Victor Yes, yes, I'll let her know.

Glazier (*to Mlle Skunk*) You see, he'll let you know. (*pause*) Don't cry.

Dr Piouk For the love of Saint Anne, let's get out of this madhouse. I'm terribly thirsty.

   Silence.

Let me invite you to dinner.

Glazier You're inviting me to dinner?

Dr Piouk Both of you.

Glazier Why me?

Dr Piouk I like to have company at my revels. Then you can take me home in a taxi.

Glazier I can't. I must look after Michel.

Dr Piouk Michel?

Glazier My son. He's ill.

Dr Piouk Well, then, we'll go and see your son first. We'll give him a little sedative. Then we'll go and have a blow-out. A gastronomic dinner: all three of us. Oysters, I've got such a craving for oysters, it's incredible!

Glazier There's nothing like doctors for dancing on people's graves.

Dr Piouk What d'you expect me to do, tear out my moustache? Come on.

Glazier (*to Mlle Skunk*) Don't cry. He'll get over it.

Mlle Skunk Adieu, Victor.

Dr Piouk Come on.

> *He leads Olga to the door.*

We'll find something else. (*He turns round.*) I'm in a period of lucidity, it's fantastic. We must drink to it.

> *Exeunt Mlle Skunk and Dr Piouk. Victor is standing as if rooted to the spot. The glazier goes up to him.*

Glazier You aren't angry with me?

> *Silence.*

I did my best.

Silence.

I'll leave you my card.

He holds out his card. Victor doesn't take it; perhaps he doesn't see it. The glazier puts it down on the bed.

Give me your hand.

Silence.

Victor!

Victor What is it?

Glazier I'm going. Give me your hand.

Victor My hand? Here it is.

He holds out his hand. The glazier takes it, shakes it, kisses it, lets go of it, and exits quickly.

Victor looks at his hand, which is still outstretched, raises, opens and looks at his other hand, sees the tablet, throws it down, rubs one hand against the other, shakes his shoes off, walks. After a moment he sits down on the bed. He sees the glass, throws it down. He stands up, goes over to the switch, turns the light off, goes back and sits on the bed again. Looks at the bed. Sees the glazier's card, picks it up, looks at it, throws it down. Straightens the bedclothes. Hears footsteps. Enter Mme Karl. She switches the light on.

Mme Karl Well?

Victor What is it?

Mme Karl Is that the way you go out?

Victor Yes, that's the way. What do you want?

Mme Karl I want my answer. Are you staying or are you going? I've got three people after the room.

Victor I'm staying.

Mme Karl Give me some money, then.

Victor stands up, searches in his trouser pocket, brings out a wad of crumpled notes, gives them to Mme Karl, searches his pocket again, brings out some coins, gives them to Mme Karl. She counts. Sound of computation.

It's a hundred and forty sous short.

Victor It's all I have.

Mme Karl It's not enough.

Victor I'll give it to you some other time. (*pause*) Take the tools. Sell them. They must be worth something.

Mme Karl The tools? What tools? (*She sees them, goes and gives them a closer look.*) But they don't belong to you.

Victor He gave them to me.

Mme Karl Ha ha. Why would he give them to you?

Victor I don't know. But he did give them to me. Take them.

He sees the glazier's card, picks it up, gives it to Mme Karl.

Here's his card. Just ask him.

Mme Karl puts the card in her pocket, gathers up the tools, puts them in the tool box.

Mme Karl Ouch, my poor back! How low can people stoop! (*She straightens up, the tool box under her arm.*)

Victor If you find the diamond, keep it for him. He wants it.

Mme Karl The diamond? Now what are you on about?

Silence.

What diamond?

Victor I don't know. It's a sort of tool, I think. Ask someone.

Mme Karl looks at him, shrugs her shoulders, starts to go out.

Madame Karl.

She turns round.

You haven't found a jacket on the stairs by any chance?

Mme Karl A jacket? What jacket?

Victor I can't find my jacket. I think I lost it on the stairs. If you find it, you can sell it as well. (*pause*) It's brown, I think.

Mme Karl Are you completely round the bend?

Victor goes and sits on the bed again. He looks at the bedclothes. Mme Karl looks at him.

Victor Madame Karl.

Mme Karl What?

Victor Madame Karl.

Mme Karl *What?*

Victor You couldn't give me another blanket, could you?

Mme Karl Why? Are you cold in bed?

Victor Yes.

Mme Karl Ah well, spring will soon be here.

Silence.

Do you want something to eat?

169

Victor No.

Mme Karl I've got some nice soup.

Silence.

A little bread and butter?

Silence.

You'll get ill.

Silence.

I shan't be able to look after you.

Silence.

How sad! (*Exit.*)

Victor sitting on the bed. He looks at the bed, the room, the window, the door. He stands up and starts pushing his bed to the back of the room, as far as possible from the door and the window, that's to say towards the footlights on the side of the spectator's box. He finds it very difficult. He pushes and pulls, with pauses to rest, sitting on the edge of the bed. It's obvious that he isn't very strong. He finally makes it. He sits down on the bed, which is now parallel to the footlights. After a moment he stands up, goes over to the switch, turns the light off, looks out of the window, goes and sits on the bed again, facing the audience, scrutinises the audience, the stalls, the balconies (if there are any), to the right, to the left. Then he lies down, turning his emaciated back on humanity.

CURTAIN